Praise for *A Rebel Chick Mystic's Guide*

"Who better to help you rock your life than an inspirational rocker chick? In A Rebel Chick Mystic's Guide, Lisa Marie Selow connects with the volume button that controls the song your soul dances to . . . and cranks it up! This is a great book if your life is crying, 'More! More! More!'"

— **Michelle Phillips,** best-selling author
of *The Beauty Blueprint*

"Anyone who thinks walking a spiritual path or healing yourself has to be boring hasn't met rockin' rebel chick Lisa Marie Selow. If you know there's a divine spark within you but you're having trouble accessing it, A Rebel Chick Mystic's Guide is your road map back home, where your spark of divinity always radiates. But don't be surprised if you find your freak flag flying high on your journey to a more spiritually connected life."

— **Lissa Rankin, M.D.,** author, speaker,
and blogger at **LissaRankin.com**

"Lisa Marie Selow's A Rebel Chick Mystic's Guide will light a fire under your bottom and get you moving toward happiness in a big hurry."

— **Lama Marut,** author of
A Spiritual Renegade's Guide to the Good Life

"If you're ready to live life out loud, let this authenticity master introduce you to the bliss of true self-acceptance! Rewrite those rules! Craft your own definition of perfect! Lisa Marie Selow provides an enlightening, effective blueprint for know... ...
yourself, as well as learning t...
voice. What could be m...

— **Lisa McCourt,** ...
7 Simple Steps to You...

A Rebel Chick Mystic's Guide

Hay House Titles of Related Interest

YOU CAN HEAL YOUR LIFE, the movie,
starring Louise L. Hay & Friends
(available as a 1-DVD program and an expanded 2-DVD set)
Watch the trailer at: **www.LouiseHayMovie.com**

THE SHIFT, the movie,
starring Dr. Wayne W. Dyer
(available as a 1-DVD program and an expanded 2-DVD set)
Watch the trailer at: **www.DyerMovie.com**

☆ ☆ ☆

*THE ART OF EXTREME SELF-CARE: Transform Your Life
One Month at a Time,* by Cheryl Richardson

*THE BEAUTY BLUEPRINT: 8 Steps to Building Your Life
and Look of Your Dreams,* by Michelle Phillips

HEART THOUGHTS: A Treasury of Inner Wisdom,
by Louise L. Hay

JUICY JOY: 7 Simple Steps to Your Glorious, Gutsy Self,
by Lisa McCourt

THE POWER OF YOUR SPIRIT: A Guide to Joyful Living,
by Sonia Choquette

*RELAX—YOU MAY ONLY HAVE A FEW MINUTES LEFT:
Using the Power of Humor to Overcome Stress in Your Life and Work,*
by Loretta LaRoche

REVEAL: A Sacred Manual for Getting Spiritually Naked,
by Meggan Watterson (available April 2013)

All of the above are available at your local bookstore,
or may be ordered by visiting:

Hay House USA: **www.hayhouse.com**®
Hay House Australia: **www.hayhouse.com.au**
Hay House UK: **www.hayhouse.co.uk**
Hay House South Africa: **www.hayhouse.co.za**
Hay House India: **www.hayhouse.co.in**

A Rebel Chick Mystic's Guide

Healing Your Spirit with Positive Rebellion

Lisa Marie Selow

INSIGHTS

HAY HOUSE, INC.

Carlsbad, California • New York City
London • Sydney • Johannesburg
Vancouver • Hong Kong • New Delhi

I dedicate this book to my late grandma, Edith, a rebel chick who passed along her wit and wisdom and love of music and dancing to me. I thank her for teaching me to be brave and speak my truth.

To my soul mate, best friend, and hubby, Jan, who has always supported me from day one. Thank you for being a fellow traveler on the spiritual path.

And to all of the beautiful, talented, loving, unconventional women out there with rebel hearts and spirits.

Contents

Preface

Who Is This Rebel Chick Mystic?

"I think most people have a natural instinct to rebel."

— ELVIS PRESLEY

Helping women to heal and move past blocks has been a calling for me for nearly 20 years as I made my journey from being an activist in the nonprofit sector and a legal assistant to working as a massage therapist, an energy worker, a professional psychic, a life coach, and a writer. My goal has been to make the world a better place one person (especially one woman) at a time. Guiding women on how to live from their spirits eventually became my focus, and I realized that I, along with many of my clients, were *rebel chick mystics*. This is my term for women who desire to carve out their own paths in every aspect of life, including spirituality. I want to begin by sharing my story—letting you know the road I've walked and how I came into my own as a rebel chick mystic.

Early Rebellions

Besides working with rebel chick mystics as a psychic and life coach, I also resonate with being one. I remember growing up questioning almost everything, feeling rebellious from an early age. Growing up in white, middle-class, Midwestern suburbia and attending a parochial school for nine years, I marveled when I met people who were different from myself. Questioning the teachers and pastors at my religious school felt fun, even though it sometimes caused awkwardness. This was my early beginning as a rebel chick mystic, challenging spiritual authority figures.

When my parents divorced when I was in elementary school (mainly due to my father's alcoholism), I wondered what could have been done to heal things. It led me on quest to understand people better, and even at a young age, I devoured self-help and psychology books. I learned that there were positive ways to heal, which seemed to always give me hope about my own life and others' lives.

As a teen, my rebellious side came out even more, as it does for many people. I purposely worked on being different from others through my clothing, musical tastes, political beliefs, and attitude. The idea of a "rebel without a cause," however, never sat well with me.

I struggled with low self-esteem, being teased relentlessly at school. I was afraid that I was damaged, not good enough, not pretty enough, not smart enough, and not skinny enough. My college days were a bit better, but I still struggled in some ways, funding most of my education myself. Living away from home for the first time, I felt free to explore things that were new to me, including various cultures, musical styles, political activism, art, and even religious paths, right along with my courses. During this time, I found my true self more, establishing my personal, more adult rebel chick mystic beliefs about life, but also falling into binge drinking and partying too much.

By the time I was 21, I became tired of that lifestyle, and around that time, I met my future husband, Jan. He supported me in believing in myself, and I was able to get my studies and grades back on track.

Finding My Path

After graduating from college, I worked as a legal assistant to see if I wanted to invest my time and money in law school. I thought if I worked within the system, I'd have the power to help create positive changes for women on a larger scale. It was emotionally draining, since many of the cases dealt with women and children who had been abused or mistreated in some way. I exhausted myself and had many disillusioning experiences. I couldn't bear the idea of earning my living under such highly stressful conditions.

I was depressed, feeling like I had wasted four years of college. I got married soon after, and my husband was very supportive of me, encouraging me to follow my heart, since he was the breadwinner. This was a godsend because I experienced serious, almost constant fatigue, along with upper-respiratory infections every six to eight weeks, no matter how much I took care of myself.

As I took a break from the corporate world in the late '90s, I became a serious mountain-bike racer and had some good results in races initially. But when I stopped improving and being able to recover from my training efforts, I knew it was time to find out what was going on with my health. I was diagnosed with chronic fatigue syndrome.

Although the doctor was a loving, integrative-medicine practitioner, the diagnosis made me angry. I was frustrated with my body for betraying me. Soon, however, I found myself rebelling in a positive way, determined to reverse the health challenges. I was on a quest, spending thousands of dollars on different healing modalities, all the while researching careers out of guilt that my husband still was the breadwinner.

I felt drawn to a career in massage therapy, reasoning that helping others would force me to take really good care of myself. Although I enjoyed the work, I wore out my joints, and then received injuries in a car accident that forced me to stop working in the field. So I cut my career short, transitioning to using energy modalities such as Reiki, Polarity, and Healing Touch.

A surprising thing happened to me while doing energy work with clients: I found myself opening up my psychic abilities. This was a part of me that I had forgotten. Growing up, my late grandma and I did things like reading tea leaves or tarot cards. I realized that I had been highly intuitive since I was very young, but didn't know what to call it or how to explain it.

The field intrigued me, so I immersed myself in studying, taking classes and reading books on psychic development. I began pursuing my own spiritual path, dabbling in meditation, yoga, journaling, and other self-care. I felt that I was returning to my true self, remembering parts that I had ignored or tried to cover up. Besides using divination tools with my grandma, in high school and college I had played around with tarot cards, giving people readings for fun. In 2005, I began giving psychic readings professionally, working with a large number of people very quickly after having given readings for free for the previous few years.

My Personal Dark Night of the Soul

During the fall of 2008, my husband, who had been working as an engineer at a large automotive company for a while, was offered a buyout—a payment to voluntarily leave his job. At the time, the economy seemed to be tanking, especially in the Detroit area where we lived, where the automotive industry is a huge part of the economy. At first, this felt like a blessing and a possible opportunity to relocate to our favorite place, Southern California.

I just assumed that my husband would look for another engineering position. Instead, he decided to get a full-time job, earning minimum wage at a bicycle shop, to determine if it really was his dream to have one of his own. This freaked me out! Prior to this, I never had to earn a substantial amount of income, so I felt incredible anxiety. We were living on our savings and what I could manage to earn on my own as a psychic. For about six months, I did a marketing push, but I couldn't make enough money.

I ended up getting a job as a psychic at a local metaphysical store in the summer of 2009 to supplement my income. Clients came to me with serious challenges such as bankruptcy, foreclosure, job loss, physical illness, deaths in the family, incarcerated loved ones, divorce, and depression. Some had more than one of these happening at the same time. In 15- or 30-minute readings, I tried to relay guidance to them as best as I could, sometimes questioning if I was really helping them, due to my fears of being in a similar situation.

My income at the store was averaging about five dollars per hour, with about 25 percent of it going to gasoline and parking. I was neglecting my own psychic business, which really made me feel depressed. It felt like my marriage was crumbling, as my husband and I fought more and more, especially about money. I worried about losing my home or having to file for divorce. At times, on my way driving to and from work, I cried uncontrollably, not sure what to do to make things better in my own life. This was the dark night of the soul for a modern mystic, I later realized.

One January night in 2010, while driving home in a serious snowstorm on my birthday, I felt like I reached the breaking point. Although I'm not a religious person, I prayed out loud as I drove over an icy bridge, fishtailing in my rear-wheel-drive car while neighboring vehicles slid across the road, telling the divine that I couldn't handle so much stress in my life anymore.

Suddenly, peace washed over me. I realized that I had forgotten my spiritual path, along with my hope, faith, and trust in the universe. It was a wake-up call for me to get back on track and find that feeling of peace once more.

Claiming Rebel Chick Mystic for Myself

Later that winter, a client named Angelina came to see me for a reading at the metaphysical store. When she sat down, she asked, "What can you tell me about my life purpose?" This question startled me, since I hadn't heard it in a long time. I was excited to help her, relaying that as I tuned in to her psychically, she was surrounded by plants, fruits, and vegetables. I also shared that I felt that she was a healer in some way, and that she'd resolved her own health challenges, which seemed similar those I'd had in the past.

Angelina confirmed what I said, explaining that she wanted to teach others about nutrition but wasn't sure how to go about it since she had a professional organizing business. I told her that I saw she could combine her two passions, since even feng shui (the Chinese art of placement) refers to how our inner and outer worlds are intertwined. She was excited about these ideas, but seemed a little worried about what others would think. I blurted out, "Do it anyway! Don't care what others think." I told her to rebel, but in a positive way by doing what her heart desired. She smiled and hugged me after the reading.

My own words hit me hard. For months I'd been sitting on a domain name for a new website that combined my psychic and punk-rock natures, but I hadn't developed it since I was worried about what others would think. I realized I had to walk my talk. I see now that this is when I really claimed *rebel chick mystic* for myself, choosing to carve out my own path. I continued to encourage my clients to do the same by making changes that felt good to them in their own lives.

I had fun developing my new site, using my creativity, flexing some major courage muscles, and even hosting my own Internet radio show. My fears of ridicule were unfounded, and like-minded clients and colleagues were easily attracted to me. In my downtime at the metaphysical store, I worked on my marketing and online content. Soon, my anxiety decreased, and my mind cleared so that I could see that I had other options for eventually becoming a breadwinner, such as getting an office job or going back to graduate school or both.

As I was investigating my options, my husband ended up landing an engineering job after a very brief search. I quit my job at the metaphysical store to focus on my own psychic business, and on my last day at work, the manager handed me a flier for a nutrition class that someone dropped off for me. I saw that the class was being taught by my client Angelina! My heart felt as though it would burst with joy, and I knew that it was truly okay for me to move on.

When I saw that I had helped at least one person, I felt as though my mission at the store was accomplished, and it was time for me to begin the next leg of my journey. My dark night of the soul had ended, and it was time to share the lessons I learned.

This is a big reason for my writing this book. I desire to help women realize that they are not alone, and that they can heal, making changes so that they can enjoy life. The thing that I want to share the most is the idea of positive rebellion, which is at the core of living as a rebel chick mystic. I'll tell you a little bit more about rebel chick mystics and explain how to use this book in the Introduction that follows, and then we'll explore positive rebellion in-depth in Chapter 1.

Introduction

Come On, Let's Go!

"I like a little rebellion now and then."

— THOMAS JEFFERSON

Ladies, let's start a loving, fun revolution to rock the world, unleashing our amazing, awesome, sassy, spirited, brilliant, beautiful, and big-hearted true selves!

In this revolution, you are in charge of your own destiny. You get to do what your heart desires, carving out your own path. You can get help along the way, and you'll probably even inspire others. An important part of this revolution, I believe, involves healing yourself (or *shifting the shit* that might still be holding you back). Your healing process will not be the same as anyone else's. Part of you might feel drawn to live your purpose more fully, or you simply might have a desire to rock the boat in your personal or professional life (or both). Wherever you are in your journey and however you feel about change is perfect. Come as you are.

Before we go any further, I want to emphasize that taking some time to heal yourself is not selfish. I believe that our healing work as women creates a wave of love that can positively affect the planet and other people. In her book *Mother-Daughter Wisdom,* Christiane Northrup, M.D., writes, "Every woman who heals herself helps heal all the women who came before her and all those who will come after her." I'm excited by the prospect of our personal revolutions creating positive change in the world.

This book aims to be like a wise friend, and is actually written with the intention to coax you to write your very own rebel chick mystic's guide, using exercises with thought-provoking questions, journal prompts, and some entertaining quizzes. It's like a playground of sorts to comfort your spirit, to really let loose, and to draw out your self-honesty—along with helping you explore and dig up your awesome, sparkly, hidden treasures from within.

Another key aspect of a personal revolution is the positive rebellion I mentioned in the Preface. It's not the stereotypical rebel path of self-destruction: being a loner and staying stuck in your angst. (Black eyeliner, fishnet stockings, and motorcycle jackets are optional. Please wear what feels best for you!) I developed the idea of positive rebellion in my work as a professional psychic while working with women who tend to have some common traits:

- Like to be in charge of their own destiny, making their own rules for their life
- Enjoy carving out their own spiritual path
- Are working on healing their lives in some way

- Feel called to help others, whether in personal relationships, at home, or in their career or volunteer work

- Tend to be open-minded about life and learning

- Feel the need to rock the boat in their personal and professional lives sometimes

- Embrace diversity

- Have sometimes experienced significant life challenges

- Understand the importance of lovingly speaking their truth

- Enjoy having outlets for creativity and self-expression

- Are considered to be "too caring" or "too sensitive" sometimes

- Have been called "bitchy" or "too assertive"

- Don't resonate with all aspects of traditional womanhood

- Identify with some of the various countercultures in history

- May be intuitive

During the course of this book, you will discover your own preferred, delightful methods of positive rebellion, as well as claim the term *rebel chick mystic* for yourself. If you identify with being a rebel, I know that you don't take too kindly to people trying to define you!

How This Book Came to Be

In my work as a psychic, I felt called to help facilitate clients' healing, not just provide them with the stereotypical information about when they would meet a tall, dark, handsome stranger for romance; inherit a sum or money; or go on a tropical vacation. From my heart, I wanted to ask spirit for empowering information so that clients could determine their own futures.

After I began to focus on this, clients started to ask me more and more for some easy-to-use tools for creating lasting transformation. My role as psychic started to shift into that of life coach. Many times, I gave clients a simple journaling exercise or two to do after our sessions. My intention was to help these individuals help themselves, rather than have them be dependent on me as a psychic to give them all of the answers and predict their fates. In fact, each chapter in this book is based on a topic that came up repeatedly for my clients.

I've been moved by inspiring stories from women I know and have worked with in my journey, and I wanted to share that inspiration as well. Stories from my own life also illustrate various concepts and let you see that I walk my talk as a spiritual teacher. I don't like to recommend healing work that I haven't done myself.

My hope is that you will learn you're not alone, and I provide resources and ideas to assist you along the way. At times, you might feel that I'm really challenging you. This comes from my strong, rocker-chick work ethic, meaning that I like to improve and get results. I'm an electric guitar player who actually enjoys practicing musical scales—this might help you understand my mind-set. Scales prepare me not only to improvise, but also to write my own songs. Personal-growth homework helps you rock out in a similar way, creating more happiness in your life. So, I don't mind working hard, but it has to be fun!

Using This Book

This book has nine chapters, each one containing some exercises and quizzes to help you to focus on healing various aspects of your life. Some of these life areas include: making your own life plan, letting go of your inner good girl, embracing your true self, finding your life purpose, and carving out your spiritual path. I respect that everyone reading this book is in a different place in life. Some have done more healing work than others. In those cases, doing additional work will just refresh or strengthen the results of your past efforts. On the other hand, you may not have done this type of work before, and this is okay. Wherever you are in your journey is perfect.

Don't feel as though you have to do every piece of homework. It's fine if you want to skip certain exercises entirely, possibly revisiting them later. Also, you don't necessarily have to read the chapters in order, but it will be helpful to take it slowly, one section at a time. Please be gentle with yourself and get some support if overwhelming emotions and feelings arise. (If you need to obtain counseling or therapy, please see the appropriate professional for your situation.)

Although healing yourself is a bit of work, it is not a race, so you don't have to rush through this book at all. But you might choose to devour it like a delicious cupcake, and that's fine, too.

Your life and what you desire can change, often very quickly. You might wish to do all of the exercises as a baseline, so that in few months or a year, you can look back and see how things may have changed. Then you can redo the ones that inspire you or help you when you feel stuck, if you feel guided to do so.

I recommend getting a journal for doing the work in this book, along with writing down ideas and about a-ha moments that come to you. Any notebook that you like is fine, and it will become your very own rebel chick mystic's guide as you complete the exercises and quizzes. In later parts of the book, you might need to gather some vision board–making supplies, such as a cardboard pieces or some corkboards, pushpins, photographs, and magazines to cut inspiring words and pictures out of. Some glitter or sparkly, colorful pens—along with some good, rockin' music—can't hurt either.

As you read, understand that when I mention terminology related to spiritual concepts, you can insert the terms that feel best for you, whether that's spirit, the divine, God, Goddess, universe, source, higher power, or something else. Also, note that the usage of "chick" in this book is meant in a positive, girl-power type of way.

Please know that my intentions come from a loving place, since I only want the best for you. It's your turn to be a rock star in both your inner and outer lives. Similar to how a lead guitar player takes center stage with her skilled, blistering solo, you too can let your creativity, gifts, talents, and inner truth shine for all to enjoy. (And you don't have to be in the spotlight unless you want to do so. Your "center stage" will differ from mine and everyone else's, and this is okay.)

It's truly my heart's desire to assist you in creating your best life possible, filled with everything that feels good to you. I see myself as an amplifier of sorts, mentoring you and helping you plug into your heart and spirit. Consider me as your courage coach that will cheer you on every step of the way.

So let's get started. Let's set your heart and spirit on fire. Courage is not needed, just a desire to move forward. (Sometimes, the courage shows up after you take action.) I'm honored to be a part of your journey.

In the first chapter, I will guide you through making a plan for your own positive rebellion. Rebel chick mystics have many options, and the main thing to remember about positive rebellion is that its goal is love. If you do things with love, especially toward yourself, you can't do them wrongly. It's that simple.

Chapter One

Plan Your Path
of Positive Rebellion

*"The only way to deal with an unfree world
is to become so absolutely free that your very
existence is an act of rebellion."*

— ALBERT CAMUS

If you're anything like me, you're itching to get started on this journey, so we'll begin by jumping right in and exploring a key theme for rebel chick mystics: *positive rebellion.* This quality sets us apart from the crowd and will be a guiding principle as we move through the different topics of this book.

I've heard many women say that they feel pressure to conform to societal norms and feel guilty if they choose a different path. It's only human to have a bit of anxiety when you start to do your own thing, but you don't have to live a cookie-cutter lifestyle. It's possible to carve out your own path with your own rules, using this key concept.

What Is Positive Rebellion?

Rebels sometimes are seen as self-destructive, addicted, lonely, angry, quiet, mysterious, pessimistic, and without a purpose. Rebellion also carries with it a history of political violence. Traditionally this energy has been forceful, trying to get rid of the existing structure or order. It has sent the message that one group is right and the other is wrong.

My approach, however, is quite different. With positive rebellion, you're choosing to do both small and big things that are loving, supportive, or helpful for yourself or others (or both). Instead of rebelling against the idea of authority, you honor your own inner authority, along with others' wisdom that resonates with you. You may start to know your own personal truth that lives in your heart. And when you practice positive rebellion on a continual basis, you'll notice that you are no longer willing to stay stuck or buy into negative or limiting beliefs, ideas, or situations. As you make changes, fear and conformity let go of their hold on you more and more.

I asked some clients and good friends of mine to describe this rebel chick mystic quality. Following are some of the ways they completed the sentence: *Positive rebellion is* . . . :

- *. . . doing what feels right for you, instead of what you think you're expected to do.*

- *. . . creating a mind-set for happiness and success, when others are more interested in the negativity and doom portrayed in the media.*

- *. . . leading with the heart, not your head so much.*

- *. . . having a glass of water while everyone else is having a beer.*

- *. . . asking your husband to do the dishes while you take a bubble bath.*

- *. . . not yelling back at someone when they yell at you.*

- *. . . giving a stranger a smile, just because you feel like it.*

- *. . . not gossiping at work with your co-workers.*

- *. . . being okay with your choices, even if others don't get it at first—or ever.*

Your own examples of positive rebellion will emerge and grow as you complete the exercises in this chapter and continue on your personal path You'll discover that positive rebellion can occur in different forms. This chapter is the buffet table I've prepared for you, presenting you with some delicious options. Consider the ideas described here as food for thought, to inspire and fuel you.

Your choices range from small, internal ones to taking action on a more global level, including activism. As you read this chapter, be sure to have your journal ready to write down any ideas that come to you. This will begin to create your own rebel chick mystic's guide.

Please know that all forms of positive rebellion have the potential to bring gifts and blessings to yourself and others—one method isn't superior to another. You don't necessarily have to take external action. You can simply mentally reject your own negative or limiting beliefs, as well as those belonging to others. Your mind-set creates your life experiences, so internal rebellion is powerful. Please do what feels right for you. (It's even all right to skip this section for now and revisit it later, if you don't feel ready for positive rebellion yet.)

Intend to Have Fun

Although much of this book will focus on healing, I want to remind you right now to have fun along the way, and positive rebellion is a great way to do so. For example, you might decide to do something different with your physical appearance, or you might make small choices each day that you consider to be outside of the box. Think about your own life and how you might like to incorporate such enjoyable changes. You might wish to write down in your journal some interesting, quirky, or entertaining ways you can rebel.

The law of attraction says that your thoughts and feelings create your life. (This subject fills entire books!) If you're having fun, chances are that your thoughts and feelings will be upbeat, so you'll have joyful experiences. But, if you don't have a positive mind-set, you might not end up creating the type of life you desire. If you're not there yet, simply *intend* to have fun. Intention is a powerful thing, paving the way for the positive results that you desire.

Shifting the Shit that Holds You Back

Sometimes I wonder if we need a blatant reminder about the benefits of having a positive outlook when we get off track. For example, a close friend of mine was listening to me rant one day. After hearing me go on and on about my problems, she interrupted me and lovingly but firmly said, "Stop your crapitude! You can shift the shit in your life!" At first, I was shocked, but soon I started to laugh. Her humorous words helped me remember that I can change my mind so that it has more positive, affirming thoughts, feelings, and emotions.

Your attitude creates your life. You might want to start observing your own thoughts and emotions on a daily basis. Not everyone does this, so it's another great way to rebel in a positive way, working on being different than the norm. Even if you're an optimistic person, it can be helpful to see whether you have limiting ideas and beliefs. Some of these might be coming from your subconscious mind's programming, which often originates in the family and in society. No matter where these limiting beliefs come from, they'll look and sound the same. Often, the word *should* is attached to them. For example, "Women who have children should stay at home, not have a job." Or they'll express a generalization, such as, "All women should become mothers." Some women believe, "I'm too fat," or "I'm too old." These might have been absorbed from living in a culture that's obsessed with youth and thinness.

Rebelling against your limiting beliefs by working to replace them with more supportive ones is definitely a form of positive rebellion in a world that can seem filled with hate, violence, and negativity, especially if you regularly consume mainstream media. Indeed, rejecting the many manifestations of limiting and negative impulses, on both personal and collective levels, is an effective way to practice positive rebellion on a daily basis.

Exercise: Eradicating Limiting Beliefs

The following exercise will help you learn about any limiting beliefs you might have, along with how to write affirmations for them. This exercise also can be an option in the future if you feel that you need to revisit an area for healing, since sometimes there are layers of emotions and feelings to process.

It might appear simplistic at first, but this exercise will really help you discover who you don't want to be. It's a strong first step in peeling back the false layers to reveal your authentic self.

First, let's work on what's holding you back:

1. Make a list of all of your limiting beliefs and ideas. Take some time with this. Dig deep to uncover everything, from the most subtle to the most ridiculous things that you've heard about what you can't do or who you can't be. Write down as many as you can think of right now.

2. Next, assign each belief to a category according to where you think it came from, such as upbringing or family of origin, institutions such as schools or church, and so on. Your categories might include areas such as society in general, career/work, popular media, or others. This will help you to see where some of your limiting beliefs originated.

3. Start thinking of the qualities that are opposite of these limiting or negative beliefs, so that you can proceed with the next part of this exercise. Write down everything that comes to mind.

Next, let's work on designing and amping up your affirmations practice:

1. On a new piece of paper, write an affirmation for each limiting belief. These are positive statements about what you can do and who you can be that will begin to

shift your thinking. Use the present tense, since your subconscious mind doesn't know the difference between past, present, and future. Avoid negative and tentative terms such as *can't, won't, maybe, might,* or *possibly,* since these can make it more difficult for you to believe that what you desire can become true.

Here are some examples:

a. For the limiting belief, *I'm too old,* avoid saying something such as, *I don't miss out on anything, even though I'm older.* Instead, you could affirm, *I enjoy every age and take advantage of the blessings that come with time.*

b. If you currently believe, *Women who have children should stay at home,* it will be less helpful to say, *As a mother, I don't need to stay at home, even though I have children.* Rather, try an affirmation such as, *I am a loving mother who knows what is best for herself and her family, and I honor my inner knowing.*

c. For an idea like, *All women should become mothers,* stay away from statements such as, *I am okay, even though I don't have kids.* Keep it positive, perhaps affirming, *As a woman, I am free to follow my own path to happiness.*

2. Circle the three limiting beliefs on your list from the first part of this exercise that you find the most challenging, the ones that you especially want to kick to the curb. The affirmations you wrote to replace these are a good place to start with your daily practice.

3. Choose the frequency and time of day to work with your affirmations. Some people do them once a day, while others find that multiple times per day works better. You can even write affirmations on small pieces of paper, hanging them in your home and work environment as a reminder to focus on the positive.

4. Speak your affirmations aloud or read them quietly. Usually, it's effective to repeat them multiple times to reprogram your subconscious mind.

5. Put some enthusiasm and feeling into this practice. Add some of your sassy or spunky attitude, if you want. Really work on believing these new ideas with your entire being.

6. Consider possibly playing some uplifting music in the background as you do your affirmations. Music can be an ally in anchoring new information into your mind (think of how children commonly learn the alphabet to music).

I did an informal survey of clients, friends, and fellow musicians and found that their song recommendations ranged from "Be Yourself" by Audioslave and "Fuel" by Metallica to the Beatles' "Good Day Sunshine" and Louis Armstrong's version of "What a Wonderful World." Choose what motivates you, be it the Ramones, Queen, or Lady Gaga.

7. After you work on your three most challenging limiting beliefs and begin feeling some shifts, you can add affirmations for some of the other negative ideas on your list, along with the ones you started with. Just honor yourself and move at your own pace.

Affirmations don't have to be complicated. To help get you started in your own practice, I'd like to share how some rebel chick mystics have gone about it. My client Rosalyn came to me for coaching, wondering how to shift her limiting beliefs about money. She discovered that she'd inherited an idea from her family of origin that she had to work hard to earn a living. She assigned this to the category Upbringing and wrote an affirmation to address it: *Money is enjoyable and easy to create in my life.* Another client, Devin, realized she'd learned in school that she had to get all of her work done before she could have fun. This was assigned to the category Schooling, and she wrote the affirmation: *I deserve to enjoy myself and have fun.* Anabelle had a fear about calling herself a healer, and she believed it came from being publicly ridiculed at her first job during her teen years. The limiting belief was put under the category Career/Work. The affirmation that she created was: *It is safe for me to be a healer, and I embrace and accept my calling in life.*

I began my own journey with affirmations back in 1998, when I was diagnosed with chronic fatigue syndrome. I refused to accept the illness, part of my own version of positive rebellion. In fact, I carried Louise Hay's book *Heal Your Body* with me everywhere I went, doing affirmations as much as I could. After using Louise's book, I was inspired to write: *I have an abundance of energy on all levels. I feel perfectly healthy in all ways!* I eventually reversed that illness using a variety of methods I previously described, along with the affirmations. However, I didn't stop living my life to the fullest while diligently working on my healing, since I continued to pursue my goals and dreams. This is important, since it might be tempting for you to focus so intently on healing yourself that you lose track of what really matters to you.

9

Stop Your Case of the "Some Days"

Your internal work is an ongoing process. Be gentle with yourself as you let go of what no longer serves you. It can feel overwhelming at times, especially if you are processing emotions and feelings that have been there for a while. But you don't have to hold off until your life is perfect to follow your dreams. Please, don't wait for "some day." That day is now! By working on yourself, you can live more fully, be your happiest, and rock the world in your own special way.

Some people wait for years before they allow themselves to take action on what matters to them. Some of my clients have delayed doing big things such as starting a business, forming a rock-and-roll band, or writing a book because they felt they weren't ready or *perfected* enough. High-achieving women often seem to have a bit of the *imposter phenomenon,* a term coined in 1978 by psychologists Pauline R. Clance and Suzanne A. Imes, which refers to the anxiety that others will find out you're not qualified to do something.

Of course, at times you may need additional education and experience, but don't feel as though you have to be an expert in every aspect of your dream. There's nothing wrong with wanting to learn and grow, but try not to procrastinate. Start where you are, with baby steps. It's totally okay to be a work in progress. As Michelle Phillips, a wise coach of mine, wrote in *The Beauty Blueprint,* "It's okay to not be okay." When I read this the first time, I felt relieved, releasing some of my own self-criticism, along with my worries about what others would think of me if I took action on my dreams and goals, instead of focusing on my roles.

Coming Out of the Captivity of Your Roles

Another way you can engage in positive rebellion is to not allow yourself to be defined by your roles, whether by yourself or others. Womanhood has become more complex in the modern era, and it can feel overwhelming. I felt a negative charge when I first heard the song "Just a Girl" by the band No Doubt. Intellectually, I knew that women had more rights than in the past, but part of me still felt the captivity that Gwen Stefani sings about. Many of us have felt restricted or even imprisoned by the multiple roles that we're often expected to fulfill, including wife and mother. Even if you're not a wife or mom—the roles traditionally associated with busyness in our culture—you still have parts that you play each day, such as employee, sister, daughter, friend, and aunt.

If these weren't enough, women also have to balance career, family, health, finances, self-care, hobbies, life purpose, and more. My client Delilah exemplifies the complexity of a modern woman's life so well. She not only takes care of an elderly relative, but also babysits her two grandsons from time to time. Besides being a wife, she owns her own catering business, does volunteer work, and keeps her house immaculate. When I asked how she fit it all in, let alone found time for anything like a long bath or meditation, she told me that she uses a reminder feature on her cell phone to help her take five to ten minute breaks here and there during her day.

Delilah isn't unique. Many articles in the popular media discuss how busy women's lives have become and the need for balance. There's a lot of talk about how women are pressured to "get it all done," along with feeling like they have to be all things to all people.

Removing Your Superwoman Cape

You might tie some of your self-worth to how tired you are, as proof that you're valuable to others. One of the biggest challenges you can face as a woman is losing yourself, forgetting who you truly are amidst all of your responsibilities. It can be really difficult to find focus on what truly matters when you're so busy, distracted, and living to please others.

You can rebel against this pressure. There's so much information out there about how to achieve balance, but I bet you laughed when I mentioned the idea. You might even be yelling at me, "What the heck is *balance?!*" It's different for everyone. For some, it might be working 60 or 80 hours per week, especially if you love your job. I used to be a competitive bicyclist, and I knew women who had children and full-time jobs along with racing—and some even competed in other sports, such as running or triathlons. I was in awe of them since I was tired from just having a part-time job while I was racing, without any children.

Consider creating a self-care program or asking for more help with your responsibilities as you rebel against any feelings that you have to be all things to all people. If you feel that you don't have time to do important things, I suggest getting up an hour earlier or cutting out an hour of television each day. This sends a message to your inner self that you're serious about making changes in your life.

Another idea to consider is that maybe after years of taking care of meals, you'll decide that it's time for loved ones to do the dishes so that you can have more time for yourself. Some of my female clients have written me e-mails excited about how they decided to hire a housekeeper to free up energy and time for other things, such as their creative endeavors and hobbies. At work, you might decide to delegate some duties and ask your boss or co-workers for help when you're overloaded. When you take steps to find balance in simple ways, it can feel liberating, creating feelings of peace within you. Even just freeing up an hour each day gives you some time to work on projects and self-care and to relax. When you address even one major stressor in your life, it can make such a huge difference, affecting other areas. You might decide to make a dramatic shift by doing something such as starting your own business so that you can gradually transition into more meaningful work that sets your heart on fire, with the ability to carve out your own schedule, including time for self-care. Or it could feel like it's time to address some larger situation that's wearing you out.

Evaline, for instance, was flying cross-country on the weekends to visit her boyfriend. Besides being expensive, it was tiring. Evaline decided that she no longer could live like this, so she found a job closer to her boyfriend that also made her heart sing. Although it might seem that she was sacrificing too much, she later said that her depression lifted when she able to have more fun and meaning in her life. It was the right choice for her at that place and time.

You might not find yourself doing something so radical—but hey, you might! The changes your spirit calls you to make will happen when you're ready, and the following exercises will help you start getting clear on the type of changes you'd like to create.

Exercise: Roll Call for Your Many Roles

Make a list of the various roles you have in your life, such as: wife, mother, sister, significant other, friend, grandmother, aunt, co-worker, artist, musician, writer, gardener, and so on. Next to each one, write down all your duties and how you're of service. Include even the things that you don't feel are significant, such as lending a listening ear or keeping everyone's schedule in order. List everything you do. It might help to think about the previous week and how things played out to get the details. Take some time with this.

If you feel tired after just reading your list, you're not alone. If you feel good, your roles could be in balance. Either way, give yourself a big hug because you do so much for others. You make such a difference. Think of this and refer to your list if you ever start to feel that you're inadequate or don't do enough to help others.

The next part of this exercise is to look at your list of roles and prioritize them. Label the most important with a number 1, and the second most important role with a 2, and so on. I hear you protesting: "But Lisa, I can't rank these things because they're all so important." I ask you to rethink this, girlfriend. You're not saying someone or something doesn't matter or that you don't care about that person or thing. You're just figuring out how to best use your energy and maintain peace in your heart. Our relationships are so important to us as women, but you can't be all things to all people, at least not all of the time.

Your priorities might change from day to day, but the underlying top three roles, once you're conscious of them, will start to influence your choices and how you spend your time. As those changes are settling into place, the next exercise will help you gain a clearer picture of how you'd like your life to look, not just focusing heavily on your roles.

Exercise: Breaking Character to Become the Rock Star You Are

You aren't just your roles. You're a woman with passions, opinions, goals, dreams, and a vision for your life. As you know, if you're taking care of others, there's the danger that you can lose parts of yourself. Let's not let that happen! Take your time and try not to hold back your inner truth as you write down your answers to the following questions:

1. Who are you aside from your roles?
2. Who's your true self? How does she act, think, dress, and live?
3. What's truly important to you in life?
4. Who do you want to be?
5. How do you want to focus your life from now on?

Once you've completed this, compare what you wrote with your list of roles from the exercise before this one. See if you notice any disparities. Look at where you might not be living as authentically as you desire. Do you still feel defined by your roles? Don't be hard on yourself if you're not where you want to be right now.

As you focus on your priorities, you'll notice that all that is not your true, rock-star self will gently fall away, leaving room to be and live as you desire. This might take some time, but allow yourself to enjoy the journey step by step, celebrating your accomplishments as you go along the path. If you're already living your inner truth and are clear on your priorities, returning to the prior exercises when you're going through an overwhelming time in your life can be helpful. I've had to do that myself, and so have countless others.

No More Psycho June Cleaver

I used to believe that I had to always meet everyone else's needs. It was exhausting, and I needed to set some boundaries. I clearly remember saying, "No more!" (Okay, I actually said "Fuck this!") I was scrambling to get dinner ready after working on my business all day. In between cooking and taking phone calls from distressed clients, I was putting on makeup, trying to look nice for my husband before he arrived home from work. As I looked in the mirror, I thought, *Who is this psycho, punk rock June Cleaver?* I was aspiring to be like some 1950s TV housewife, even though my husband never expected it from me and I'd abhorred that stereotype since I was very young. There I was, multitasking on the phone—something I preached to my clients to avoid.

This was an opportunity to rebel in a positive way by no longer defining myself according to my roles. My spirit was trying to get my attention so that I'd get back on track with my priorities of self-care, working on my hobbies, and just relaxing and having fun in general.

There seemed to be a cosmic two-by-four hitting me on the head, since that very week I had more than a few female clients expressing similar realizations. Jillian had started her own graphic-design company to be at home with her children, but she told me that she was feeling challenged by being a stay-at-home mom. She enjoyed being with her kids, but in some ways, she said, it was more stressful than having an office job. It was more difficult to fit her work in during the day since the kids were taking shorter naps. She'd started using her limited free time to keep up with client projects. Her husband worked many hours, family members lived too far away to help out, and they felt too strapped for cash to hire a babysitter.

We discovered that Jillian volunteered to help others so much that it became a detriment to herself. She even did free graphic design for friends. She realized that she needed to change something, but she wasn't sure where to start. For homework, I gave her the exercises in this chapter so that she could become clearer on prioritizing with her roles, and then begin saying no as necessary.

Exercise: Where Do You Need to Say No?

Many women need to work on learning to say no to some of their demands so that they can say yes to their priorities. Answer the following questions in your journal as honestly as possible. Think about the people you tend to help out the most, along with whether it's draining or energizing. Consider the areas where you might need to say no more often.

1. Do you overcommit yourself?

2. When someone suddenly needs your help, do you drop everything and help them? Or do you get back to them later?

3. Do friends and family always turn to you for advice and support? Are you their free counselor at times?

4. Do you volunteer for everything at work, socially, or with organizations you belong to?

5. Do you find yourself doing a lot of favors?

6. Are you ever frustrated when you need something and there's no one to provide it?

7. How does asking for help make you feel?

These questions will get you thinking about boundaries. If you find that you're tired, drained, and resentful as a result of helping others, it might be time to look at scaling back your commitments, learning how to say no, and being more directly honest in a loving way with those who request frequent help.

Rehearsing saying no prior to the actual conversations is beneficial. My clients report that it makes their interactions with others less stressful. I recommend using a direct, short, and unemotional statement, something like this: "I'd love to help you, but at this time, I'm unable to do so due to prior commitments." You'll feel how rebellious and positive this is from the moment you first try it.

Learning to set boundaries can help you free up more energy and time to pursue your dreams, hobbies, and self-care. Some women like to do volunteer or other charitable work, but talk about how it's a challenge to fit such things into their already busy lives. The next brief section is a good place to start, revisit, or prioritize your volunteer or activist work.

Be a Rebel with a Cause

Activism isn't required for rebel chick mystics; it's only mentioned here as one way to rebel against the negativity in the world. You might choose to stand up against poverty, war, or pollution, for example. Although some spiritual teachers say that you ought to focus on the outcome you desire, rather than what's upsetting in the present, you might not be able to do this right away. It's possible that your emotions will act as a catalyst; and once you get going, you'll be able to describe the condition of the world and those you are helping with much less anger, frustration, and sadness. You could say that you're "helping feed people" instead of "feeding the hungry," "creating world peace" instead of "fighting war," or "healing the environment," instead of "fighting pollution."

The way you frame things can be powerful. Mother Teresa reportedly was asked why she wasn't politically active, especially against modern wars. She's said to have answered, "If you have a rally *for* peace, I'll be there." This idea was so powerful to me that it catalyzed me to write and teach further about positive rebellion.

But as you know, finding the time to dedicate yourself to a cause can feel challenging. Part of you might really want to make the world a better place, but you may be overwhelmed by the idea of adding more things to your schedule. One option is to start small. Even actions such as writing letters to government officials or spending an afternoon cleaning up garbage at a local park make a difference. You also can donate small amounts of money to your favorite causes and charities.

It's possible to find enjoyable and simple methods with activism. In her book *Tranquilista,* Kimberly Wilson discusses creative ways to give back, such as going on a volunteer vacation, using blogging and social media to bring awareness to your cause, mentoring others, hosting food or clothing drives, and starting your own nonprofit. It can also be fun to partner with friends and colleagues.

Rest assured that if this seems like too much, you can choose to take action later, or you might not feel called to be an activist at all. Whatever choice you make, if it aligns with your priorities and keeps you on the path of positive rebellion, it's the right one for you.

Exercise: Putting Together Your Positive Rebellion Plan

It's now time to officially write down your plan as part of your rebel chick mystic's guide. You've done some important homework to get clarity on which limiting beliefs you need to heal, your priorities, and where you might need to set boundaries, along with starting to explore the truth of who you are. Look back at everything you've written for all of the exercises so far. Using what you've learned, answer the following questions:

1. Which areas of your life do you want to rebel against the most? Some of the countless possibilities include: your own limiting beliefs, social stereotypes, identifying yourself through your roles, your upbringing, and injustice in the world.

2. Of those areas, which one or two do you feel are most important for you to start with?

3. How do you personally define *positive rebellion?*

4. How do you want to engage in positive rebellion in your own life? Write down everything you can think of.

5. What are you going to do to take care of yourself? List a few ideas for starting your own self-care program. It's okay to start with small actions such as doing some journaling

in the morning or taking a ten-minute break at work. Start with one or two things per day, and then you can add other methods later on, as you get used to the idea of taking time for yourself. This will help you ease out of devoting most of your free time to your roles.

6. What sets your heart on fire? Write about your passions. Answer the question: *How can I rock the world in my own unique way?*

7. Extra credit: How can you use your gifts, skills, and talents for making the world a better place as a rebel *with* a cause?

The things that you write down here are part of your own rebel chick mystic's guide. This is the good stuff! It's inspiring to have this information on hand when you feel lost, stuck, or unsure of yourself. If you ever feel as though you've forgotten who you are or what matters to you, get out your answers to the questions in this chapter. Look at what you've written when you've had the type of bad day that makes you momentarily question yourself, especially if someone has said something to try to pull the rug out from under you. What you wrote here can serve as a naysayer repellant.

And if you have a bad day now and then, it's okay. Just try not to dwell in the negativity. It can be helpful to put aside your need to be perfect with your personal growth. There is no unseen force grading you on your performance. The next chapter will help you stop being so hard on yourself, and you'll learn about how you're perfect in the eyes of the divine. You'll also define the term *perfect* for yourself. It's powerful to rebel against other people's and society's definitions so that you can create your own rules that support you.

Chapter Two

Be Your Own
Version of Perfect

"Perfectionism is self-abuse of the highest order."

— ANNE WILSON SCHAEF

So far, I've discussed rebelling against your own ego, limiting beliefs, being defined by your roles, and putting others first. You've started to create a plan for your path. This chapter helps bolster this plan so that you have even more confidence in yourself.

Even if you already have a strong sense of self, you still might find that you're affected by society's notions of perfection. Rejecting the idea that you need to be perfect according to external standards is another act of positive rebellion. In the Western world, popular culture perpetuates perfectionism, especially for women, and especially when it comes to physical appearance (one of several areas we'll look at in this chapter). Images of airbrushed female bodies send a message to women of all ages that they should strive to achieve the same look. Entire industries prey upon women's insecurities about appearance.

Magazine headlines scream, "How to Have Flawless Skin!" and "Get Your Bikini-Ready Body in Three Weeks!" I've even seen ads for plastic surgery while in public bathroom stalls. It can seem as though there's no escape.

While it can be empowering to look and feel good, there's a fine line between this and basing self-worth on physical appearance. In her book *The Beauty Myth*, Naomi Wolf talks about how women's magazines are considered the authority on what is acceptable for women in popular culture, not just when it comes to appearance, but also for life in general. If you regularly consume popular media, you might notice an underlying common theme that females should conform to the accepted ideal standards of beauty and lifestyle.

Besides feeling pressure regarding their physical appearance, many women are pushing themselves to uphold society's standards of female perfection in other aspects of life such as school and work. There's an idea that started during the modern women's movement in the 1960s that we could have it all, meaning a family and a high-powered career. While modern women have been working toward career success and pay equality, increasing our opportunities in the working world, many of us have still found that we're doing the majority of the housework and child rearing. Things seem to be shifting slowly, with more men adjusting their roles to help women out at home. But a 2008 study by the University of Michigan showed that having a husband creates seven extra hours of housework per week for wives (while having a wife saves a man an hour of housework per week!). Perhaps we have a ways to go when it comes to achieving balance.

If you feel like you're on a quest to be perfect (or feel guilty perhaps because you're not), you are not alone. Please don't despair. It's possible to change your mind-set.

Just by questioning things, you can start to create a new paradigm for your life that is positive and empowering.

Exercise: Perfectionism Where Are You Now?

If you have perfectionist tendencies, you might be striving toward standards set by others. Write your answers to these questions in your journal to see where you stand.

1. What are you striving for?
2. Are you truly happy?
3. Does all of your hard work help you feel as happy as possible?
4. Do you feel as though you can live according to your priorities? Or do you still feel like you have to do it all—all by yourself? (You might want to look back at what you wrote about your roles and priorities for the previous chapter's exercises.)

Look at the answers to your questions. You might discover that you are happy and living the life you desire. If so, that's wonderful! These questions are meant to be a gentle check-in to see where you are right now or at any given moment. If life becomes hectic in the future, you might wish to revisit them.

To the Beat of Our Own Drummer

Rebel chick mystics often struggle with the parts of traditional womanhood that don't resonate at the heart level, and the pressure to be perfect makes matters worse. Defining for yourself what it means to be a woman is a rebellious act, and you might feel as though you're left out or not represented. The popular media, our mass consciousness, and the corporate world don't always recognize the needs of women outside the norm. There may be messages that you're flawed or strange. People might try to sell you products or services that you don't really need, promising happiness that might not fit your definition and priorities.

There are many ways to express being female. Some women choose not to have children, not to work outside the home, or not to get married. Many don't desire men romantically, instead preferring women or both women and men. Modern women dress, behave, work, and live in a myriad of ways.

It might be difficult for you to imagine that you can be really happy living according to your own definitions. Have you ever attended social functions and wanted to hide under a rock because of the standard questions that people ask you when you first meet? You usually hear these familiar phrases:

- What do you do for a living?
- Are you married (or in a relationship)?
- Do you have any children?

Sometimes these questions spring from natural curiosity, and sometimes people don't know what else to ask. Whatever the reasons, the inquiries primarily address your roles and can trigger doubts about whether you're living up to expectations. You might start to compare yourself unfavorably to the person you're talking to, especially if their roles are conventionally seen as more important.

If you're outside the norm in some way, you might even wonder what others think of you.

I know that I sometimes cringed at others' silence when I mentioned that I had no children (and didn't plan to, most likely). Usually, this came up in conjunction with my working at home. I worried that people would think I'm a slacker, that they were wondering, *What does she do all day?* since I hadn't chosen motherhood or a traditional day job. Eventually, I stopped worrying so much about what others thought of me, enjoying my path much more.

It's possible to exhaust yourself attempting to live up to other people's expectations, and I encourage you to discard any beliefs that don't fit you. You can make this positive rebellion official by creating your own definitions of womanhood and other major concepts. (If you enjoy traditional womanhood, however, that's fine. You still might create your own definitions.) In the following exercise, you will come up with your own definitions of womanhood and the other main aspects of life.

Exercise: Formulating Your Own Definitions

It's your life and you get to decide what its various aspects mean. This can be very revealing and clarify your path, blowing away the need for false perfection.

Get out your journal and write down the answers to these questions, really taking your time with each one:

1. What does it mean to be a woman in your eyes?

2. When you were growing up, what did the women in your life teach you about what it

means to be female? Which teachings were the ones that served you the best?

3. What are your definitions for the following concepts: success, life purpose, happiness, health, abundance, friendship, family, and love?

4. Write down your own definition of perfect. What does perfection mean to you?

5. Do you feel that your definitions from the first four questions are different from society's? What stands out the most for you?

6. How do your ideas of womanhood and other life aspects fit into your path?

You could be excited about finally identifying what these important ideas mean to you, or you could be feeling a bit overwhelmed that your ideas don't converge as much with the norm. If you already strongly identify with being a rebel, you might see this as a good thing. You're capable of thinking for yourself and aren't willing to live like a robot on autopilot. Rebel chick mystics tend to be willing to live outside the norm, at least a little bit. But the extent to which you do so is up to you.

Soaking Up the Love and Good Vibes

Do you know that some great spiritual teachers say that you are already perfect in the eyes of the divine? I too believe that spirit loves you and wants you to be happy while here on the planet. This idea might be shocking if you grew up in a traditional religious setting and learned about how much you were a *sinner*, needing to be perfected by asking for forgiveness from God, that angry white guy in the sky.

Part of being a mystic is finding the spiritual path that works for you, which we'll look at more closely in Chapter 9. For now, I invite you to consider aligning yourself with how wonderfully the divine sees you.

The idea that you're perfect might be difficult to embrace first. It might even be tough to accept simple things like compliments or expressions of love from others, if you struggle with perfectionist tendencies. You might think, *Oh, that's not really true,* when someone tells you that you're beautiful or talented. Although you might not believe in seeking outside approval to enhance your self-esteem, you still can honor the part of you that enjoys those loving words.

Here are some ideas to help you to embrace your *perfect* self:

1. In all of your e-mail accounts, create a file called Love. Archive the kind notes and compliments that you receive from others, referring to them when you need a lift.

2. Create a file of compliments. Cameron Tuttle, the author of *The Bad Girl's Guide to Getting What You Want,* writes about making a "compliment bank." She recommends that you create a small index-card file with categories for each of your positive qualities. Every time someone gives you a compliment, write it down on a card and put it into the compliment bank. You can refer to them to bolster your mood and self-confidence, and foster positivity in your life.

3. Notice expressions of love from others. Absorb their affection into your being, basking in the good vibes. You

might even write the details down in a love journal, a physical version of the e-mail file.

When you doubt yourself or feel down, looking at the expressions of love from others reminds you that you're divinely perfect. The universe uses messengers at times to get its points across. The important message it's trying to convey is that you're so very loved by others and the divine.

This idea that you're already perfect still might be hard for you to digest, and it's okay if it takes a little while for you to start living by your own definitions. It can take some time to find your footing. But once you do, you'll be able to fly—and kick some butt, if you want to!

Exercise: Just the Way You Are

As women, we often are far too humble. Perhaps you've been taught that bragging is not "ladylike" or that you shouldn't draw attention to yourself by singing your own praises. It can be beneficial to kick these ideas to the curb in order to bolster your self-esteem and self-confidence, replacing them with the idea that you are *awesome!*

In your journal, write down the ways in which you're already perfect. I recommend referring to your personal definition of the word. Please try not to be so darned modest! If you have difficulty tooting your own horn, think about writing these things from the perspective of the divine. If you worry that you're not worthy enough to do so, try writing from the perspective of someone who unconditionally loves you, such as a parent, grandparent, or romantic partner.

Give yourself some time with this exercise. If you need to, come back to it at a later time. It's okay if you can only think of a few things right now. I understand how you might feel. I had to learn some challenging lessons to stop being so hard on myself.

Embracing My Own Perfection

Before I learned that the divine sees me as perfect, I took some pretty drastic measures in the name of self-improvement. I reasoned that I needed to purify myself in body, mind, and spirit in order to be of service to others as a spiritual teacher. I tried everything from hours of yoga, meditation, and affirmations to chanting mantras and journaling volumes. I worked on cleansing my physical body with herbs and colon hydrotherapy sessions.

Some sources I studied at the time said avoiding caffeine, sugar, alcohol, food additives, and other substances would help me open up more spiritually. I wasn't really eating a lot of animal products, and only occasionally using small amounts of caffeine. But I was driven to be *perfect* and decided to embark on a raw vegan diet, following all the other restrictions, too.

I felt great the first few months of eating this new way. Soon after, though, my health began to deteriorate. I asked for advice from people on the raw vegan message boards I'd been frequenting. Some said that I was just detoxing and that I'd feel better soon, once all of the toxins were out of my body. I believed this for a little while, until I saw the data from my training for bicycle racing and discovered that I wasn't recovering from my workouts very well. I even had a slight relapse of chronic fatigue syndrome for a short time, too, but I persevered since this was supposed to be the perfect way to eat. After a couple years on this diet, I'd developed some new symptoms of severe inflammatory intestinal issues from eating raw nuts and seeds and was feeling very weak. When I look at pictures of myself from that time, I can now see that I looked pale and deathly, even more so than in my high school Goth days.

My huge wake-up call came one morning as I sat on the edge of my bed after the alarm clock went off, in so much stomach pain that I wondered if I should drive myself to the doctor or just go straight to the emergency room. I had healing work scheduled that day, and the healer's acupuncturist friend just happened to be in town, so I received acupuncture and Chinese herbs to get my health back on track. Soon after, a friend who's well-versed in Ayurveda and yoga helped me understand my body's needs more. I slowly added cooked food back into my diet, including some occasional animal products. In a short time, I regained my strength, stamina, vitality, and sanity. My digestive and organ inflammation healed, too.

My raw vegan friends seemed to drop out of my life since I was no longer following the diet. It felt like I was a failure and being judged. I thought I'd scream if I heard the slogan "Cooked food is poison" one more time. Even eating half of my diet raw wasn't considered "successful." I wondered if it would be easier to meet such strict standards if I were living in an ashram in the mountains, without having to drive a car in gridlock traffic, go to a job, or deal with the other complexities of modern life.

The most difficult thing for me in all of this was the idea that there's only one right way or best way to live, and that someone else was defining perfection. Fundamentalism isn't fun, whether it's related to dietary or other belief systems. The main issue that I have is the judgment. If you condemn others for their lifestyle choices, it negates the higher vibration you're seeking. Whatever works for you is perfect, and it will be different from what's best for others.

Recovering from Perfectionism

Deciding to honor my body's messages and needs, I ended up feeling much happier and healthier. The mind can be the best healer, and whatever you believe will come true for you. Spiritual teachers of diverse backgrounds have been saying this for many years. I smiled once when I went to a lecture by a visiting Buddhist monk, and the event organizers brought the monk a Starbucks cup. I knew that this was a teacher for me, especially since I thought he embodied what he taught about the principles of moderation (or "the Middle Way"). I like to enjoy a good cup of coffee (and a beer) myself, now and then.

Easing up on yourself is a good idea. When you focus on what's wrong with your body or life, obsessing about what isn't perfect, it seems to create a block and keep you from becoming the real you. It's okay to incorporate order, healing, and spiritual connection in your life. Working to balance your perfectionist tendencies doesn't mean that you stop trying to improve yourself, but you can choose to make the changes in a more gentle way. You can be loving and accepting, embracing your humanity and your gorgeous spirit.

A sense of humor can also be helpful in diffusing your perfectionism, I've discovered. One time at a psychic fair, a client asked me some questions about her health. She worried about whether she was normal since she only slept five to six hour per night, instead of the seven to ten hours suggested by a women's magazine. She was also concerned that she was only having one bowel movement per day, since she'd read on a health website that three was the normal number. I lovingly asked her to define *normal*, inviting her to consider that perhaps the best standard is defined by each individual. (Of course, I always tell clients to seek a professional opinion if something seems really out of the ordinary for them.)

My stories from my own life and from those of clients might seem extreme, but I'm hoping that we can all laugh at ourselves about how it's possible to go a bit crazy on our healing and spiritual paths. We're all learning, and we can learn from each other, helping each other learn how to not beat ourselves up so much.

Exercise: Stop Beating Yourself Up

If you still feel as though you're continuing to hold yourself to an unrealistic standard, the following exercise can join your love file and compliment bank as a tool to help you to gain more insights into how to shift this habit into the positive.

The video for the song "Perfect" by Pink inspired me to create this healing exercise. The video shows a young woman struggling to love herself, along with scenarios that depict the various ways some women tend to be hard on themselves. Pink sings about stopping the negative self-talk, changing it into thoughts of self-love.

Take out your journal, and answer the following questions. It might help you to consider whether you'd talk to a good friend in the same way that you talk to yourself.

1. Do you compare yourself to others?

2. Where are you hard on yourself? Write down a list of the ways you are overly critical of yourself in one column.

3. In a column directly next to your list, write down the more positive way to view what you're criticizing. Replace the negative items

with your beautiful qualities, strengths,
talents, and gifts.

I'll give you an example to get started on your own.
One common criticism might be, "I feel fat." Your positive replacement could be, "I have beautiful muscles from
working out," or you could write, "I love my body."

When you feel like you're being hard on yourself, look
at your positive list. You might even take a dark-colored
marker pen, crossing off all of the negatives, to give yourself the physical sensation of releasing these from your life.
This will help you remember that you've learned to how to
shift the negatives into the positives. You can release your
perfectionism, although it can take practice. You might
not get there overnight, and that's okay.

When you doubt yourself, beat yourself up, or feel the
need to chastise yourself for not being perfect or measur-
ing up to societal standards, review the tools of positive
rebellion and exploration that you created in this chapter.
When you embrace your individuality, you are more likely
to love yourself, and you might feel the need to be perfect
(according to external definitions) less frequently.

One particular area that's part of striving for perfection is the idea that you have to be a good girl, which
we only touched on briefly in our discussion of the traditional definitions of womanhood. The next chapter will
assist you in letting go of and positively rebelling against
your good-girl tendencies, so you can truly embrace being
a rebel chick mystic.

Chapter Three

Subvert Your
Good-Girl Persona

"Well-behaved women seldom make history."

— LAUREL THATCHER ULRICH

I walked into the dance studio a little nervous. It was the summer of 2010, and I had just awoken from my dark night of the soul (actually much more than a night—some of the hardest years of my life). I sat on the floor with the other women, chatting before class started. I stared down at the bright red, patent-leather high heels that I'd brought with me, wondering how I would walk in them. In the distance, I saw feather boas and other interesting props. The wooden floors reminded me of a yoga studio, as did my attire, but I was there to take a burlesque dancing class.

This was out of my comfort zone. I usually spent time and money on things like meditation or yoga classes, not learning the classic art of striptease. It all felt a bit *naughty,* subversive toward my inner good-girl persona. I shuddered to think about what people in my life might think if I told them I was taking this class. Yet it just felt like fun to be in this group of women, supporting each other in owning our body confidence.

I think that when you've lived through a crisis, your spirit calls you to recognize and heal any leftover issues. It becomes impossible after a while to maintain that charade of saying, "Oh, I'm fine. Everything is okay." You might be able to fool people in your life for a bit, but you can't trick your spirit. My higher self called to me to address my self-esteem issues in a fun, creative way, rebelling positively by taking the burlesque class.

When the teacher had us practice sauntering and strutting, I cracked up. I couldn't stop laughing because I recalled my years of parochial school, where we were told to walk like a *lady*. It felt healing to giggle at all of that old programming about how good girls were supposed to act. My feminist nature didn't even react negatively to the idea of learning how to take off my clothing seductively. Instead, it was empowering. Burlesque felt like a creative form of art with the costumes, dance moves, and music selection. It seemed like a celebration of the female form, as well as being playful in its fun mockery of popular culture and gender stereotypes.

After years of trying to address my self-esteem issues, I never imagined that these classes could transmute my angst about my body, and especially my turmoil over feeling like I always had to be a good girl. I laughed out loud when I thought, *Oh, my gosh, I am learning how to be bad.* I had explored this idea in my early years, like many young women, but never with any seriousness. I never really flaunted my sexuality much and sometimes worked on being more tomboyish or androgynous, wearing T-shirts and jeans as my standard uniform. But at this point, something felt really delicious about sequins, feathers, red lipstick, and glittery eye shadow.

The burlesque class illuminated that what I needed to strip off the most was my good-girl mask. It motivated me to look more in-depth at whether I was living authentically. As an introvert, I sometimes didn't want to advertise the fact that I was different. Yet my spirit was calling me to continue reclaiming the real me. I'd been a punk rocker since my early teens, and I didn't see a need to hide this any longer by trying to look, act, and dress in a stereotypical, professional, or nice-girl way when it came to my personal and professional lives. I always attracted clients, colleagues, and friends who were rebels in both their appearance and attitudes anyway.

I realized that I'd been setting aside my own needs. My good-girl persona was running the show. Heck, even getting a speeding ticket for going five miles per hour over the speed limit seemed to create enough guilt in me to last years, and addressing it with feathers and sequins was just the first step. I decided to do some more work, and it's contained in the exercises in this chapter so that you can benefit, too.

Take Off Your Mask

Carl Jung talks about the idea of personas, the masks that people wear out in the world to hide the true self. In spiritual writings, these masks are considered to be aspects of the false, or lower, self. One of the personas that some women wear is the good girl. It's most common in childhood, but aspects of it can be carried into adulthood. This plays out in different ways, but perhaps most commonly in people pleasing. You may work hard to make everyone else happy, while consciously and unconsciously tabling your own needs. You might not be able to bear disappointing anyone. I can relate.

Taking off your good-girl mask is another form of positive rebellion. Wearing that persona too much can make you easy prey for those who want to take advantage of you—your skills, talents, compassion, and time—and you could risk becoming depressed or even physically ill. In her book *Why Good People Do Bad Things,* Debbie Ford talks about the need to be honest about this, saying, "Good Girl types often do not find the motivation to change until they have exhausted themselves by trying to prove how perfectly good they are or have suffocated themselves inside the confines of their masks." (There's that idea of perfection you've been addressing.) Over time, your resentment may become overwhelming. You might even feel as though you have lost a part (or even all of) yourself.

In its more extreme form, people pleasing can take the form of loving others too much, such as in codependence. In *The New Codependency,* Melody Beattie talks about how some people who are caretakers are relieved when they get ill because it feels freeing to have an excuse to take care of themselves or receive care from others. It's important to not allow yourself to get *that* exhausted. When all of your energy, time, and effort is placed on helping others, it is very difficult to live as the real you and find the time to pursue the things that make your heart sing. So start peeling off your good-girl mask, beginning with the next exercise.

Exercise: Peeling Off Your Good-Girl Mask

As you know, part of the rebel chick mystic path is becoming more aware of where limiting patterns and beliefs came from, and then, reprogramming your mind to aid in your positive rebellion. Having worked on perfectionism in the last chapter, it's easy to see why it can be tiring to fear disappointing people or worry about having them get mad at you. You might be extra tired if you do all that you can to avoid conflict, feeling like you're walking on eggshells. And even if you don't feel like this persona is a problem for you, it's still beneficial to look at whether any of your past programming is affecting you today.

Take your time with this exercise, really delving into what you've heard and absorbed in your life. Some of it may have been buried in your subconscious mind for a while. These negative beliefs might not go away overnight, but you can continue the work you began in Chapter 1, reprogramming your subconscious with positive ideas instead.

Use your journal to write down your responses, and notice how they intersect with the work you did examining your ideas about simply being a woman.

1. Think of all of the stereotypes about good girls. Make a list by completing the sentences "Good girls always . . ." or "Good girls don't . . ." Being aware of these "rules" will help you see their absurdity. Your list might include sentences such as these:

- *Good girls always make the bed each morning.*
- *Good girls don't show any cleavage.*
- *Good girls don't make waves.*
- *Good girls always put others first.*

2. Think about the things that you picked up from parents, authority figures, teachers, the media, peers,

and society. Write about all of the ways you've been pro-grammed to believe that you need to be a good girl. You might have had adult authority figures telling you to be-have, had parents rewarding you according to their defini-tion of *good,* seen negative portrayals of "bad girls" in the media or in books, or felt the need to fit in with and obtain approval from peers.

3. Write down all of your limiting beliefs around being a good girl. Perhaps you're even worried about an unseen force catching you "being bad," or you identify with some of these examples:

- *I have to clean my room so that I won't get into trouble.*
- *I need to dress like a lady.*
- *I need to be nice all the time.*
- *I have to make sure everyone is happy.*

4. Next to each limiting belief that you wrote down in the last step, write the positive belief you'd like to replace it with, remembering the guidelines about affirmations from Chapter 1 (positive, present tense, and no disclaim-ers). For example, if you absorbed the idea that good girls don't raise their voices in public, you could affirm, *I ex-press myself easily, freely, and openly in all situations.* It's okay to write from the perspective of your younger self. In the spiritual realms, linear time can be tweaked. You can go back and replace those limiting ideas with new ones that carry forward into the present and future.

I assure you that you're not the only one working on shifting your good-girl persona. I've observed many women doing their own personal healing work in this area. Yet sometimes we don't take action because a belief is so ingrained that we think we have to continue on the same exhausting—and often damaging—path.

When you're stressed and worried, you might find that your inner good girl gets unleashed again in a misguided attempt at self-preservation. Some women recall being extra-good girls when they were younger by helping out at home or excelling in school and sports. In their minds, they were helping to prevent issues from arising within the family. When you're an adult and this persona kicks in as a defense mechanism, it can cause you to push yourself hard, with the reasoning that if you're good, no one can criticize you. My friends and I have discussed feeling at times as though there's a large group out there waiting to pounce on us, telling us all of the reasons why we are deficient in all life areas. These critics aren't real, but we can sometimes give away our power to them. Many women even worry about what the neighbors will think as they begin to be true to themselves. (Trust me, the neighbors have their own issues to work out.)

Doing your self-growth work, such as taking off your good-girl mask, is not another opportunity for you to attempt to be perfect. In addition, please know that there's nothing wrong with being a nice person, as long as you feel good about it. One positive thing, whether this mask is a problem for you or not, is that most likely you care about people very much.

Creating a new mind-set can seem to be an overwhelming project, even with the tools you've developed in the previous chapters. It can be helpful to simply see it as something you gradually create by handling each moment in a more empowered way. When developing a new habit or skill, it can take some practice to get used to doing things differently, and you may experience setbacks, such as the mask reappearing when you feel threatened. Be sure to be gentle with yourself as you slowly change your outlook.

Exercise: Starting to Shift Your Inner Good Girl

You deserve to take care of your needs. Even if you're good at setting boundaries, there might be one area that still sets off feelings of guilt for you. You can get out your journal to write down your responses to the following questions:

1. Do you feel that your inner good girl runs the show more in your relationships, love life, career, health, or another life area? Do you feel that she's in charge of more than one area?

2. Does it ever seem as though your inner good girl is running your entire life? When do you tend to feel this way?

3. What can you do right now to start setting more boundaries? If this feels challenging, you might focus on how to obtain knowledge and skills, such as taking an assertiveness class, reading some books on communications, or get some counseling.

4. Write down small action steps that you can take each day to start practicing speaking up. You might ask your family to help you with the laundry so that you have time for hobbies or relaxation. Or you could start

taking a lunch break at work instead of eating at your desk.

5. Create an action plan for the next three weeks, outlining how you will start to shift your inner good girl. Some sources say that it takes 21 days to acquire a new habit, but please be gentle with yourself if you discover that's not enough. It's okay to need a longer amount of time. For each day of the 21 days, assign yourself one of the steps you wrote down in step 4.

Be sure to attend to your well-being on all levels as you do this exercise. After you take your action step of the day, you might want to write about what the results were and how you felt. It can be helpful to journal about your emotions each day, since it's common to experience a few "growing pains." You might want to enlist a trusted friend for support, and you can even choose to do this exercise together in order to help each other through any possible rough patches via a daily e-mail or telephone call. Or, if you feel you need extra support, you can do this work under the guidance of a professional counselor.

Remember that you don't have to complete all exercises in this book, and you can also return to them later on, when it feels right for you. It's significant just to start waking up each day and consciously refusing to live according to any stereotypes about what it means to be a good girl. If that resonates and you don't feel like making an official action plan, you might want to use the next exercise option.

Exercise: Crank Up the Volume of Your True Self

Here's another option if you don't feel ready for a 21-day challenge. (You can still do this exercise, of course, even if you're working through those three weeks.) Have fun and try not to hold back as you fill in the blank for each of the following statements.

- *If I were to dress as the real me, I'd wear . . .*
- *I need to set boundaries with the following people in my life . . .*
- *I really need to speak up more in my life about . . .*
- *I want to express myself more through these creative avenues . . .*
- *People don't know that I'm really . . .*
- *The music that inspires me to be my true self the most is . . .*
- *I desire to have more of the following qualities . . .*
- *Right now, I need to rebel against . . .*
- *If I started to take better care of myself, it would feel and look like . . .*
- *If I could behave in any way that I desired, I would . . .*

If you ever feel overwhelmed and lose sight of your true self, you can refer to these statements in your journal to help you to get back on track, reminding you of who you truly are.

Finding Support and Sisterhood

You've done a lot of work on yourself so far. At this point, you might feel as though you need a break. That is okay. Be sure to honor your needs. Getting support from others can be a challenge at times, especially for those working to subvert their inner good girls, and you may not feel you can ask someone in your life to help you. At times, support can come in the form of positive energy. This means that you don't necessarily need to enlist actual people in the flesh to assist you with your healing process or other parts of your journey. You're a mystic, after all, so you can call upon other forces and energies. These can assist you with feeling strong and courageous, and you won't feel so isolated.

You are not alone. There have been many women in history who have made waves, not behaving themselves and kicking their inner good girl to the curb. Many of these rebellious women rocked the world with changes. You are made up of the same genius, but the fear of the unknown sometimes can prevent you from moving forward. If you find yourself feeling this way, ask yourself if you're taking on others' anxieties. By finding sisters of the heart who have moved past fears, you can quiet any external voices that might be playing in your head. You can harness the energies of your own heroines of the past and present to help guide and inspire you.

Personally, I admire the strength of Joan of Arc, who led the French army during key battles of the Hundred Years' War, although I prefer not to be burned at the stake for heresy. I respect the courage of Rosa Parks, who refused to give up her bus seat to a white passenger in Montgomery, Alabama, becoming the symbol of the civil rights movement. I'm inspired by the American abolitionist author

Harriet Beecher Stowe, who dared to write about the conditions of African-American slaves in her novel *Uncle Tom's Cabin,* bringing awareness to the social issue of the day. Mary Magdalene of the Christian Bible has always given me courage. Even though some labeled her as an adulteress and prostitute, she is still considered an influential disciple of Jesus.

From modern times, I resonate with the author Naomi Wolf, who wrote *The Beauty Myth,* which helped fuel the third wave of feminism in the United States. She continues to write and speak, along with being politically active. Another one of my heroines is Wanda Jackson, considered by many to be the first woman to record a rock-and-roll album. She paved the way for women in the male-dominated music industry, bringing some feminine sass and sexuality. I highly admire Joan Jett, especially since I'm a female guitar player and singer. After her band the Runaways broke up, Joan went on to create a long-running, successful career in the rock-and-roll genre, refusing to give up, even though many record companies rejected her music at first. Joan led the way for other female musicians and singers, inspiring them with her edge and talent. The artist Pink also speaks to me, not only with her music, but especially with her activism in the areas of animal and human rights.

You probably already draw inspiration from some historical and contemporary women. The following section—featuring a quiz, a meditation, and an exercise—will help you find additional role models for help on your path.

Quiz: Who's Your Rebel Chick Mystic Mentor in Spirit?

This is a divinatory way to find some mentors, women you can study and learn from, especially when you need assistance with your own healing, don't want to feel alone, or desire additional courage and support. Of course, you might not be able to meet and work with these women in person, but you can call upon their strengths to express through you. They are mentors in spirit.

For the following, place a check mark by the descriptions that resonate the most with your heart. You might find that you connect with each one, but try to pick the top three that inspire you the most. At the end, I will provide an answer key that tells you which women the descriptions correspond to, but please, don't look ahead until you've selected the three statements that feel best to you. Be sure to research the women that you resonate with, even if they're familiar, so you can learn more about yourself.

1. *I like the idea of writing, creating art, using humor, or making music about personal and social issues to bring attention to them.*

2. *I would find it exciting to disguise myself as someone else or break gender stereotypes to get information or education, to fight in a war, or even to start a revolution or liberate others in some way.*

3. *I like the concept of being a pioneer, someone who's the first to do something.*

4. *I prefer the idea of protesting in person, even if I risk arrest or contending with violence.*

5. *I'm attracted to passive resistance: meditating, praying, sending love and energy, doing affirmations, and feeling peaceful to make change in the world.*

6. *I like the idea of using teaching and speaking as a vehicle to educate people about social issues.*

7. *I prefer to get into the field and work hands-on for causes and with people I want to help.*

8. *I like to use my attitude, appearance, or sexuality to express myself and to create change in the world.*

9. *I think it's a good idea to work within institutions and companies as a secret system buster.*

10. *I resonate with the idea of being a spiritual leader or modern mystic, here to make a difference in the world in a variety of ways, such as healing others, speaking, writing, or volunteering for causes.*

Answer key: Each number below corresponds with the descriptions' numbers above. Each numbered section has a list of women you mind find to be kindred spirits. Note that some women might fall into more than one group in your mind (and feel free to embrace other categories, too).

1. Joan Jett, SARK, Betty Friedan, Yoko Ono, Maya Angelou, Erma Bombeck, Joan Baez, Alice Walker, Anne Frank

2. Joan of Arc, Gloria Steinem, Willa Cather, Eleanor of Aquitaine, Harriet Tubman, Gertrude Ball

3. Wanda Jackson, Amelia Earhart, Marie Curie, Edith Wharton, Sandra Day O'Connor, Madeline Albright, Margaret Sanger, Wilma Mankiller

4. Rosa Parks, Angela Davis, Susan B. Anthony, Emmeline Pankhurst

5. Pema Chödrön, St. Thérèse of Lisieux, Helen Keller, St. Teresa of Avila, Coretta Scott King

6. Naomi Wolf, Sojourner Truth, Margaret Mead, Elizabeth Cady Stanton, Rigoberta Menchú

7. Princess Diana, Harriet Tubman, Mother Teresa

8. Madonna, Mae West, Janis Joplin, Bettie Page, Jane Fonda, Lady Gaga, Cyndi Lauper, Erica Jong, Cleopatra, Eva Perón

9. Hillary Clinton, Corazon Aquino, Golda Meir, Eleanor Roosevelt, Margaret Thatcher, Indira Gandhi, Catherine the Great

10. Louise L. Hay, Doreen Virtue, Marianne Williamson, Byron Katie, Caroline Myss, Oprah Winfrey

Don't let these names overwhelm you. It's not always easy to be a pioneer, to speak up, or create something to move people to change. You might resonate with the quote from Jodie Foster at the beginning of Jennifer Read Hawthorne and Barbara Warren Holden's book *Diamonds, Pearls & Stones:* "Normal is not something to aspire to, it's something to get away from." On the other hand, it's up to you as a rebel chick mystic to decide how far you'd like to take your positive rebellion, and it's okay if right now, your focus is simply exploring the personal challenges that you've discovered by doing the exercises in this book. You don't need to command an army or headline a rock concert to experience growth or make a difference, even if that's what your spiritual mentors have done.

Meditation: Downloading Some Mojo

After you research and study the women above who resonate with you, think about the many women who have influenced you positively. These women can be living, deceased, famous or not, relatives, friends, acquaintances, or teachers. Write down all of their names. Next to each name, write down the positive, inspiring, or kick-ass characteristics about each one that you love. After you complete your lists, take some time to think about how each of these traits is present within you, too. This can assist you in increasing your own *mojo* or self-confidence.

I invite you to try out the following meditation to help you claim all of this goodness that others are mirroring to you. You might wish to read through the meditation once or twice before beginning.

> *Sit in a comfortable place and take some deep breaths. Close your eyes, imagining the amazing women who have influenced you with their greatness. Some are mentors; some are role models. Imagine all of these women in a circle with you in the center. See them sending you love from the heart. Feel yourself soaking up that positive vibration. Ask the divine to shower you with these spirits' blessings. Simply sit in a receptive state, asking the divine for the characteristics and essences of these lovely women to be expressed through you. Ask to have it all manifest in a way that honors your own uniqueness. Breathe in these wonderful energies. Open up your heart to receive. Ask the divine to show you how to use your gifts, skills, and talents in a way that feels best for you. Thank these women and the divine for guiding you on your path.*

As you come back to a more aware state of consciousness, grab your journal, writing down any insights or guidance that came through for you.

Exercise: Keeping Your Rebel Chick Mystic Mojo Stoked

Now that you have a list of women from your own life and history to inspire you as you cast aside the good-girl mask, along with some guidance that they've provided, you might wish to take action to ensure that they'll continue to stay with you as time goes by. Being a rebel chick mystic, you'll come up with your own methods, so the following are just some ideas to get you started.

1. When you are faced with challenges, feel fearful, or are even just having a bad day, call upon the essence of your female role models to flow through you. Ask the divine to allow these energies to support you with decisions, get past your obstacles, or bring you the qualities that you require for the situation at hand. If you prefer, you can even select one person from your list who has certain helpful traits for your specific situation. You might be looking for patience, wisdom, courage, strength, creativity, intuition, eloquence, leadership, logic, sexuality, grace, fierceness, honesty, authenticity, or other empowering characteristics.

2. Use humor to help you shift your mind-set to be more positive when emotions challenge you. You could ask yourself what a certain heroine or role model would do: "What would Aunt Grace do?" or "What would Yoko Ono do?" This momentary humorous focus pulls you out of yourself and allows you to realign according to the qualities you value most. You'll be able to take action from a more peaceful, empowering place.

3. Place reminders of role models in your home and work space to help keep them in the forefront of your consciousness. You could create a special vision board with photographs and quotations from both the famous women you admire and your personal role models. It can serve as a visual reminder of your own greatness each time you see it. If you prefer, you can create an altar or other sacred space to honor these inspirations. Besides using photographs or quotations, you can add personally meaningful objects that represent your strengths, accomplishments, goals, and dreams—your true self. You can meditate at this altar or simply enjoy its energy as you pass by it each day.

4. Use your creativity to make new personal objects to remind you of the women who can help you. You could create a t-shirt, necklace, bracelet, scarf, painting, sculpture, or other work of art, inspired by one or more of the women you admire. If you happen to have a gift from a relative, friend, or mentor whom you admire, this is wonderful. You can work on feeling the good vibes from that particular woman as you wear or look at the item. For example, I own my deceased great-aunt Liz's pearls, and when I wear them, I focus on feeling her sense of humor. Since I wear the necklace on dressy occasions where I tend to be shy at first, it helps me remember to not take things so seriously.

5. Create a separate inspirational journal for yourself. When the muse appears, write down insights, further guidance, or information from your role models that makes you smile. Or use your journal to write letters to the individuals you admire, asking for help, support, or guidance, or simply to share your thoughts and feelings. These

aren't necessarily the type of letters that you mail. You don't have to allow the people to see it, since it's for your own healing purposes. When you look at what you wrote later, you can reflect on what solutions or ideas possibly appeared in your life after writing the letters. Or you can see where you might need to obtain support from others in your life.

These methods can help you get in touch with the support and love around you and help create that energy for yourself. As you move beyond your good-girl persona, you're not meant to be alone. You *are* allowed to be supported and loved. I give you full permission!

When you feel isolated, you can feel as though you're invisible, too. As you become your true self and heal your spirit, you will notice that it becomes brighter, and you'll start to realize that you are not meant to hide. The next chapter will help you become more comfortable with being seen and being heard, which is an important next step after peeling off your good-girl mask. And if you're already okay with being noticed, you'll discover ways to unleash more of your courage.

Chapter Four

Be Seen and Be Heard

"Life shrinks or expands in proportion to one's courage."

— ANAÏS NIN

Some women are socialized according to the cliché, "Little girls should be seen and not heard." Although I've mentioned this topic before, it can be such a major issue for adult women that it needs more attention. As a punk-rock music fan, I enjoy the X-Ray Spex song "Oh Bondage, Up Yours!" which is singer Poly Styrene's legendary response to this limiting idea. In this chapter, I'll help you find your own response.

Some women grow up being told to be quiet or to make themselves scarce. I can relate, since I had some negative experiences that later affected my self-expression. I grew up attending a parochial school, where if you talked "out of turn," your name was written on the chalkboard. Besides the public humiliation, you had to write sentences, and if you were a multiple offender, you received a check mark by your name, adding to the number of sentences you had to write. This made me prefer the written word to speaking at times. I also used to love to sing in my grade-school years, and was even a member of the church choir. My classmates ridiculed me when I didn't hit notes perfectly, however, which has affected me as an adult musician. I've worked to reclaim my voice, trying to become more comfortable with allowing others to see and hear me sing as I play my guitar. I was also criticized for the way I dressed during my high school years, and I was well into adulthood before I felt comfortable being seen by others.

Such childhood experiences can prevent women from sharing their voices, even when they have something important to say in their families, at work, or in the world at large. I've worked with some female clients who were teased relentlessly at times for the way they dressed, talked, or behaved. Have you have ever experienced similar hurts?

Although you're an adult, you might still feel worried that you'll suffer negative consequences for being seen and heard. Perhaps this originates in our cellular memories since there are many examples of powerful women being hated, ridiculed, persecuted, or even killed for being authentic, including Cleopatra, Joan of Arc, Marie Antoinette, Tz'u-Hsi, Aung San Suu Kyi, and those involved in the Salem witchcraft trials in America. Even today, women are often criticized for being "bitchy." But it's vital to live as a powerful, authentic rebel chick mystic.

Stand in Your Strength

When healing fears about being seen or heard, remember that you are no longer a little girl. Start to work on seeing yourself as a powerful woman instead, and know that you now have a choice as to how you respond to the nay-sayers. You don't have to allow them to hurt you, and you can speak up for yourself, if necessary. In *Put Your Big Girl Panties On and Deal With It . . .* , Roz Van Meter puts forth an interesting idea: obtain custody of yourself. This idea is powerful, as it not only implies taking care of yourself, but also being in control of your mind. You become your own authority, deciding what's best for you. Listening to and trusting yourself instead of others is another act of positive rebellion.

You can manage how you respond to people and life's circumstances. If you've been traumatized in the past, you might initially find your inner little girl coming out. She could be frozen or respond from a child's perspective. I recall being very young when a grown-up asked, "Who do you think you are?" after I described one of my dreams. This question is not that uncommon, sadly. Well-meaning adults try to protect us, but it still hurts. At least now you can respond differently when someone asks you to play small. With practice and support, you can start respond-ing from your adult side.

Interestingly, some women get the courage to speak up after trauma, tragedy, violence, and other crises. You may not want to hold on to secrets any longer. You might also want to share, to see if other women have experienced the same thing so that you don't feel so alone. Personally, I also hoped that sharing my own stories would give others the courage to speak up, too.

Speaking up could be part of the healing process, helping you let go of the past. Getting things out in the open may mean that they may take up less real estate in your mind, heart, or spirit. In my experience, talking about things that happened to me didn't feel scary or uncomfortable—not as much as the incidents themselves.

Additionally, if you don't manage the pain of the past, your self-confidence can suffer, and you might be more likely to put your dreams on the back burner, so the world won't benefit from your contributions.

You might consider beginning by talking things out with a professional counselor or a trusted friend. You can also release negativity through the act of writing about how you feel. This helps you gain more clarity and remember that you're a different person today than you were in the past. Work with the exercises in this book that help you reframe the past. Creating a new reality for yourself via affirmations can help cement a positive view of yourself.

Quiz: Where Are You Feeling Unseen and Unheard?

I give you full permission right now to do what makes your heart sing and to live your life the way you see fit, speaking up and being noticed. Let's begin by taking a look at the areas where you might need a little work when it comes to being seen and heard with this quiz.

For the following statements, choose true or false. Pick the response that fits the best for you. Answer as honestly as you can, but remember, there are no right or wrong answers. This is a tool to help you understand yourself more.

1. *When my boss gives me another assignment at work, I simply take it on, even though I'm swamped.*

2. *I would like to express myself creatively (through art, music, writing, or the like), but part of me worries about what others will think.*

3. *I prefer to have others make decisions for me at times, especially my partner or spouse.*

4. *I am excited by the prospect of being creative,
    even though I am busy or even tired.*

5. *I like to discuss options with family members
    so that we can arrive at a mutually agreeable
    solution or plan.*

6. *I'm scared at times to say what I think or feel
    since it might make others angry or upset.*

7. *When I feel others aren't listening to me, I see
    it as an opportunity to educate them, bringing
    understanding to the relationship and situation.*

8. *I prefer to write my feelings and thoughts down
    in a journal rather than trouble anyone with my
    problems.*

9. *I have a support system of friends who allow me
    to express myself, where I feel comfortable to be
    the real me.*

10. *Many people don't realize that I have many skills
    and talents. I prefer to keep these things to myself
    and close to my heart.*

11. *Even when family members bring up painful
    subjects, I prefer to respond in a healthy,
    balanced way.*

12. *I like to create for myself, and I don't need to
    share my creations with the world to feel happy
    and fulfilled.*

13. *At times, I want to speak up at meetings, but I
    keep quiet to keep the peace.*

14. *If someone hurts me, I express the way it made me
    feel in order to help them understand me better.*

Answer key: For each of the statements above, I have some food for thought for you to consider, depending on your answers. Also, please note the life areas in which you're not feeling seen or heard.

1. If you answered true, you might want to think about learning how to delegate. If you're not sure how to do this, check out a few of the many books on the subject or take some courses on assertiveness and communication in the workplace.

2. If you answered true, it might be time to stop worrying about what others think! Your inner critic may be getting the best of you. Try to take small steps until you're out of your comfort zone. Get support from loving friends, family members, a romantic partner, or a professional such as a counselor or life coach.

3. If you answered true, you might want to think about expressing your ideas, thoughts, feelings, and opinions more. If you want to make your wishes known to someone you love, it will be okay since you are safe with them.

4. If you answered true, you're acknowledging your human side, but are still motivated to let your passions fuel your life. If you answered false, it might be time for self-care such as resting or spending time on your hobbies or projects.

5. If you answered false, don't beat yourself up. You might be learning how to communicate or assert your needs. This is okay.

6. If you answered true, remember that it's normal and natural to feel this way at times since you're human. Also, you can't control how others respond or react. If you speak from a place of love, you can't do it wrong.

7. If you answered true, you're on your way to healthy communication and boundaries. If you answered false, see yourself as a work in progress. You are learning how to express your emotions and feelings, and this can take some time. Be gentle with yourself.

8. If you answered true, think of how you might be depriving others of giving to you. It doesn't inconvenience people to listen to and support you.

9. If you answered true, you have such a gift—treasure it. If you answered false, start taking baby steps to create this. You could do something as simple as having a monthly potluck at your house, inviting like-minded, supportive women; or you could start an online support group. It doesn't have to be difficult or time-consuming.

10. If you answered true, you might need to learn how to toot your own horn. You're modest. It's okay to share yourself with others, especially those you love.

11. If you answered true, can you come over and help me learn how to do this? Seriously, you are amazing. If you answered false, either you're choosing to not respond or don't know how to do so. Family members are your teachers, but you might not feel like you always want to address the lessons directly. Perhaps you might read books,

talk to a trusted friend, go to a support group, or write in your journal to gain perspective.

12. If you answered true, your confidence is great. But I invite you to start sharing a little bit more of your work so that the world doesn't miss out on what you have to offer.

13. If you answered true, you might resonate with the idea of being a peacemaker. This is okay at times since your healing energy or presence makes a difference. Chances are, when you do talk, people listen. If you answered false, you might be more direct or express yourself more, which gives others permission to do the same. This is powerful, too.

14. If you answered true, you are a brave soul. This is not always easy. If you answered false, you're still strong. You just might process your emotions and feelings differently from someone with a direct approach. Whatever choice you make is okay, as long as you feel comfortable with it.

Exercise: Speak Up, Sister!

Even if you already tend to make yourself heard in many ways, you might notice by doing the following exercise that some other areas call to you. Whether you feel like taking action right now or not, you can record your answers for possible use in the future. It's up to you. Think about what you learned in the last quiz, and take out your journal to write down your responses to these prompts.

1. List the areas or situations where you feel you need to speak up more.

2. Write down how you'll start expressing yourself, what you will say, and what support you need. Sometimes it's challenging to know what to say. It can take practice to get it to feel right. Writing it down can be helpful, or you might choose to rehearse what you're going to say with a trusted friend. Remember that taking action one step at a time helps expand your comfort zone.

3. Think about whether you feel called to speak up for a larger cause or even on a global level. If so, do the same process with the causes that matter to you. Create an action plan to implement your ideas one step at a time.

The Price of Invisibility

Speaking up is not required for rebel chick mystics. It's simply an idea to consider on your path. But a tendency to hide, not wanting to be seen and heard, can cause you pain. When you feel different from others, you might not feel like fully participating in life. What realizations are coming to the surface as a result of thinking about the questions in the last quiz? Is there a part of you that's a bit tired of these patterns? It takes so much energy to hide and hold in your beauty, creativity, and greatness since they long to shine through. Your spirit sometimes tries to get your attention, to get you to come out of hiding. When you see others living their dreams, following their passions, or even just having fun, you could find yourself thinking, *Oh, I wish I could do that, too!*

It's helpful to continue becoming aware of your patterns so that you can start to shift them. During my healing career, I've observed some recurring statements that rebel chick mystics make about of their fears of being seen and heard. When you read through them in the following list, have your journal handy to record anything that arises for you.

- *I feel invisible, like no one is listening or noticing me.*

- *I don't feel like I fit in anywhere in the world.*

- *I feel tired from trying to be someone that I'm not.*

- *I'm afraid to express myself creatively.*

- *I feel uncomfortable expressing my sexuality.*

- *I feel like I'm the cheerleader or support system for others, but don't receive that in return.*

- *I feel as though I live through others and their dreams.*

- *I don't have confidence or believe in myself at times.*

- *I sometimes prefer being alone, since I feel safer to be the real me.*

- *I get stuck in my head at times, not sure how to take action.*

- *I ignore my body sometimes as a way to escape reality or my dreams or goals.*

If you resonate with some of these, do not worry or be hard on yourself. You don't need to change your personal nature to be seen and heard, so honor your communication style, whether you are introverted or extroverted.

It's okay to feel nervous about what others might think. When you take small actions steps over time, you expand your comfort zone, coming out of your shell a bit more. Some women say that the courage tends to show up after they've taken action.

Being Noticed: The Starter Kit for a Sparkling Spirit

The next list is filled with ways to explore being seen and heard while you gain strength and momentum. Taking small steps and getting support will help you embrace being your sparkly self more. Write down the items that appeal to you in your journal, or use them as inspiration in creating your own methods.

1. Find a place of belonging, your own tribe. Create a safe group where you can express yourself, whether you share your ideas, emotions, feelings, creative works, hopes, dreams, or worries. This can take many forms such as a support group, social club, creative project circle, or online message board. You also can draw strength from people such as a life coach, loving friends, and supportive family members.

2. Take care of yourself. When you feel tired, it can feel more difficult to express yourself. Be kind to your physical body by eating healthfully, drinking plenty of fluids, exercising, resting, sleeping your preferred amount each night, and creating time for some fun.

3. Express yourself creatively for the pure joy of it through endeavors such as music, art, writing, or the like. Try not to put extra pressure on yourself to make things perfect. You can create to make *yourself* happy, not others.

4. Practice enjoying your sexuality in ways that are fun for you. If you're not sure how to do this, look for resources such as books, classes, or counselors to get you started.

5. Work with a life coach, healer, or counselor if you feel stuck. Sometimes it's helpful to have others' perspective, guidance, and support, since it can be hard to be objective about your own life. Having someone to report to can make you more accountable.

6. Express yourself in some small way each day. You can write in your journal or sing in the shower or while driving. You might even take a class in areas such assertiveness training, public speaking, or improvisational comedy.

7. Work on improving your communication skills. This will help you express yourself more effectively so that you feel seen and heard by others. Find resources that resonate with you in the form of books, classes, or counseling.

8. Laugh every day. When you're having fun, your heart is open, and you can worry less about expressing yourself.

If It's Done with Love, You Can't Do It Wrongly

One of my teachers always said that if you express yourself or your inner truth from a place of love, you can't do it wrongly. Energy follows intention, so if you have a positive purpose, good things will come about. However, some women seem to use their voices at times to apologize over and over to various people in their lives, which can indicate they're coming from a place of fear or shame.

Instead of apologizing, we can rebel and use our energy and words to speak up in the areas where we feel called. When you speak your truth in your personal and professional life, it can help other women in a positive way, since we're all connected. Your action is felt in the universe, giving others permission to do the same.

The world needs teachers and leaders right now on all levels. If thinking about being a leader intimidates you, that's okay. Sometimes, even the smallest gestures can make a huge difference. Maybe you'll speak up at a work meeting about something that has been bothering you or your co-workers for some time. You could attend a city-council meeting to voice your concerns about bullying in schools. You might speak out when you learn about someone mistreating another person. Perhaps you'll write a letter to the editor of a local newspaper about the importance of recycling, or you might stand up for yourself when another person is mistreating you. One individual can make a difference.

"But I'm Still Scared"

It can feel scary at times to pursue a path of being seen and being heard. When you're anxious, ask a loved one to hug or listen to you or be your cheerleader. Sometimes we bring up others' insecurities, mirroring where they need to take action, make changes, or be more authentic. You can shift the way you view criticism, seeing it as a sign that you're doing what is right for you. I've heard some talented women say that the more successful and visible they became, the more others protested. Colleagues and I have talked about how getting a critical e-mail used to set us back temporarily. But instead of getting upset, we now prefer to bless the person who wrote, since it means that we must be living our truths more fully.

Try to remember that you will be okay as you go along your path. You might wonder how I know that. I'm speaking from my personal experience; I don't like to teach what I haven't gone through. In describing my own life, I hope to inspire you to continue stretching. I've done things to express myself that were initially scary, including hosting my own radio show, taking guitar lessons in a male-dominated guitar shop, taking singing lessons, writing very honestly in my blog, speaking publicly, and writing this book. I've lived to tell about all of it.

Prior to this, I had severe fears about putting myself out there for the world to see, but it became physically painful for me not to express my inner truth. My ovaries started to speak really loudly to me with debilitating pain during my late 30s. I cracked up when my friend mentioned, in a conversation about my resistance to being seen and heard, that I needed to get some *balls,* since ovaries are the female equivalent. She was right, and I knew I needed to listen to that humorous guidance.

Over time, my pain significantly lessened as I expressed myself more. You also can have healing transformations as you take the small steps to slowly widen your comfort zone. Seriously, if I can do this stuff, anyone can! When you have success, it will fuel you, reminding you that you can do what your heart desires.

Rocking the World

You're not meant to play small or be hidden. You're really meant to rock the world! We need you to shine and let your gifts loose. I mean that from my heart to yours. You can speak, teach a class, write a blog, sing, play a musical instrument, draw, craft, paint, garden, bake, cook, and much more. Of course, I also advocate breaking gender stereotypes—maybe you prefer to work on cars, do home improvements, invent things, or tinker around. All expressions are good since they come from your true self, which is part of the divine. So let's create a brief outline to assist you on your path.

Exercise: Planning to Amplify Your Greatness

1. List the various areas and projects that you would like to work on to express yourself even more. Take your time doing this, listing every possible idea that you can think of, whether big or small, without holding yourself back.

2. Write down next to each idea the resources and support that you will enlist for your journey. You will be amazed by the tools you already have.

3. Pick an item or two from your list, developing a plan to implement them. By taking action, even in small ways, you'll be well on your way to finding and claiming your voice.

4. After you get going with the initial items, pick one or two more, repeating the process.

Now that you have tools and a plan to assist you as you step out in the world, it's time to anchor your self-confidence. This is a process, and just like anything worth pursuing, it takes practice. I prefer to approach improving confidence from a fun place. Since I'm a musician, I find that music is healing, and it also helps you learn and remember. Think about how kids are able to learn the alphabet using a song, and it's easy to remember the products being sold in commercial jingles. Music is powerful, and it's time for you to harness that power.

Exercise: Write Your Own Sassy, Confident Theme Song

1. In your journal, write down the qualities and characteristics that make you a wonderful woman. List things that you would like to believe about yourself as well as facts. If this is challenging, you might write down how loved ones would describe you.

2. Using some of those words and ideas, write a theme song for yourself. Use your creativity and don't be afraid to be sassy. You can be serious or not. You can add actual music, too, if you feel like it. This will be a something that you can sing or just read the lyrics when you find that you need a boost.

3. If you feel stuck, you can temporarily use a song written by someone else as your personal theme. Pick something that's positive and inspiring for you. If you use an mp3 player, you can check your most played songs to get some ideas.

My own sassy, confident theme song is a work in progress, but I'm pretty sure one of the lines is, "She kicks butt, speaks her truth with love, all while wearing a smile and her Ramones T-shirt." (See, it doesn't have to rhyme!) Your song is for you alone, so don't feel pressure to make it perfect. Like mine, yours might be a work in progress. There's no rush.

I'd love to see your song. Visit my website, **www .lisaselow.com**, to share it. Maybe we can create a community soundtrack for all rebel chick mystics. Our songs can be a catalyst to rock the world. Because sometimes, to make your mark, you may need to rock the boat a little bit. The next chapter is going to help you to get ready to do just that.

Chapter Five

Rock the Boat

"Do one thing every day that scares you."

— ELEANOR ROOSEVELT

One thing that I've seen as a theme for many women, including clients and friends of mine, is a tendency to not want to rock the boat that can linger even after the good-girl mask is gone. But I have to tell you: your boat can handle a little rocking. Even if you feel like your ship is sinking, it's temporary—and, of course, there always are lifelines or lifeboats (or surfboards to ride to shore in style), if you look for them.

While you may have made a lot of progress internally and in shifting negative patterns that affect only yourself, you might worry the most about how your important relationships will be affected if you start making waves. I've given thousands of psychic readings to women, and I've noticed that many have concerns about how their changes will affect their spouse or partner, friends, and children. I've heard clients say things such as:

- *I have to wait until the kids start school.*

- *I have to make dinner each night.*

- *I have to wait until the kids graduate.*

- *Once my husband is retired, then I'll be able to.*

- *I'm too busy as a mom.*

- *My friends won't like me doing that.*

- *What will my parents think?*

- *My partner won't approve.*

As you can see, you are not alone if you worry about these sorts of things. My client Carlotta was a very talented writer. She wanted to start publishing some very personal articles and blog posts, but wasn't sure how to find the time. She seemed afraid to rock the boat, worrying that others might have to adjust their schedules to accommodate hers, even fretting about what her parents would think of her as a grown adult! Carlotta could have become more of her true self by taking significant steps as a writer, but stopped herself because she didn't think others could handle it. This breaks my heart, and I don't want you to be afraid to rock the boat in your life.

Honor that you're human with fears or worries from time to time, but don't let that stop you. I'll be taking you through some work in this chapter to help you examine your fears around this particular issue and create an action plan for gentle, but possibly profound, changes in your life. Let's start by looking at where some of your worries are coming from.

Quiz: Where Are You Worried about Making Waves?

For each statement, select the answer that best describes how you'd respond or react. Answer as truthfully as you can. There are no right or wrong answers. You're simply learning more about yourself.

1. You get an opportunity to start your own business on the side. Your first reaction is:

   a.   *I'm not qualified to do that. Besides, I don't have time.*
   b.   *I'm worried—what will my co-workers or friends think of me?*
   c.   *I don't have time because of my duties at home.*
   d.   *I'm not sure about this idea. It wasn't common for women to do this when I was growing up.*
   e.   *I'm excited, and I want to learn more.*

2. You want to get back into a hobby that you had when you were younger. It really calls to you, and you can't stop thinking about it. You have this thought running around in your mind the most:

   a.   *I don't know if I still know how to do this. It's been years.*
   b.   *What will people think about me? Will they think I'm too old?*
   c.   *My spouse will think that I've really lost my mind.*
   d.   *It worked for me back when I was a kid because I didn't have so many responsibilities.*

e.   *I am going to start doing this hobby again, even if
     I only have 15 to 20 minutes a day.*

**3. Your friend asks you to go on a trip with her for
fun, but it's for one week. Your first reaction is:**

a.   *I don't know if I can justify this. I really need to
     save my money.*

b.   *What will my boss think if I take a week off from
     work?*

c.   *I am not sure I can find a babysitter.*

d.   *I don't have time to take a break since I'm so busy
     at home and at work.*

e.   *I'm interested, and I'll check my budget and
     schedule. I can make this work.*

**4. You get a promotion, but it will require relocation.
You worked really hard for this, but didn't realize that
moving was a requirement. Your first reaction is:**

a.   *I'm not sure I'm ready for this big change yet.*

b.   *What will my friends think if I up and move?
     Won't they miss me?*

c.   *I'm not sure I can do this to my significant other
     since s/he is so successful at work right now.*

d.   *I don't know about this. Maybe I should stay close
     to my family geographically?*

e.   *I am excited by this job opportunity, even though
     it makes me a little nervous.*

5. A client asks you to do some work at a discount. You've done this before, but it really drains you, and you're already overbooked. Your respond by:

    a.   *Agreeing to do the work, even though you're tired.*

    b.   *Worrying that if you don't help, the client will speak negatively about you behind your back.*

    c.   *Working late, feeling guilty that you aren't able to go home and cook dinner for your family.*

    d.   *Rationalizing that it's good to work hard, even at a discount. It's what your parents did.*

    e.   *Telling the client that you're not able to help at this time and offering some referrals.*

Answer key: If you answered mostly a's, your fears about rocking the boat might be coming from a mild case of low self-confidence or low self-esteem. Work on bolstering your belief in yourself. Chances are, you have rocked the boat before and have lived to tell about it. Make a list of the times you created changes for the better. You might revisit exercises about bolstering your self-confidence from earlier in the book.

If you answered mostly b's, you might be overly concerned about what others would think. You really are never too old to make changes, try new things, or go for your dreams. If you worry about what the neighbors will think, you continue to hold yourself back. It's your life at the end of the day. No one else can tell you how to live.

If you answered mostly c's, you care deeply about the people in your life. Yet children and spouses will live if they don't have you to cook and clean. Friends and other loved ones are here to support you. If they really care for you, they will adjust and help you. It might take some work to get them there, but it's worth it since these are your goals and dreams that we're talking about, along with your inner peace and happiness.

If you answered mostly d's, some of your socialization might be affecting you—just don't let it run the show. Become aware of it, and work on changing your beliefs, one step at a time.

If you answered mostly e's, you have a pretty healthy approach to making waves or changes in your life. You like to research things, think about them, and talk to others before you leap. You most likely are a good example of courage to others.

Use this information as a tool to understand yourself better. When you're aware of why you might be afraid, it helps you see where you need to do some work. As I discussed at length in the last chapter, fears often dissolve when you take action in your life to stretch yourself outside your comfort zone. I'm not advocating that you leap into a pool filled with sharks or jump out of an airplane without a parachute. Being afraid to do those sorts of things is healthy, since your reaction is there to keep you safe.

Instead, I'm talking about the anxieties you have about becoming more of your true self. Really, most of these end up being untrue. You tend to inherit ideas from others, including parents, friends, family, institutions, or society, as we've explored in other chapters. Some people prefer to play it safe, but you can choose differently. The next exercise will help you remember that you don't have to listen to those voices any longer and that it's safe to make changes in your life.

Exercise: Navigating Your Course

1. In your journal, make three columns. In the first one, write down all of your fears about rocking the boat. Even if the worry feels insignificant, write it down.

2. In the next column, beside each fear, write down some benefits that may result if you do decide to rock the boat. Seeing them on paper can make it clear how unfounded some concerns may be.

3. In the third column, write down an example of how you've overcome each fear in the past.

For example, let's say that you're interested in starting up a daily morning yoga practice. You're afraid that if you do this, you might rock the boat by bothering others in your household who are still sleeping. Your mind gets busy, thinking about some of the other reasons you can't do it, such as waking up earlier or getting ready for work faster in the morning. You write all this in the first column.

In the second column, you can write down the benefits of the change. You might feel more focused for your day after doing yoga, sleep better at night because of reduced stress, or improve your self-image.

In the third column, list examples of how you have received support in the past from others and were able to fit something new into your schedule in the past.

Refer to what you wrote for number three when any of your fears crop up. Sometimes your resistance shows up when you're working on making changes. This is a natural human reaction to change, and another perfect opportunity for positive rebellion. Looking at how you've overcome your fears in the past will remind you of your strength and courage.

What a Woman Needs

Although the overall result is positive, asserting your personal needs can often rock the boat. These needs can include receiving emotional support, getting more help on a project, having time to yourself to relax, receiving physical affection, having someone listen to you talk about your day, enjoying more fun activities, or performing fulfilling work. Women tend to worry about what others in their lives will think, say, or do if they even mention what's required for them to grow and flourish in their personal and professional lives.

Before we get to the next exercise, I want you to be prepared for the fact that at times, you may feel as though you have to meet your own needs. You might worry that you've exhausted everyone in the past who helped you, so you don't want to rock the boat by asking again. Or you might be in transition—such as in a new job, location, or relationship—and be anxious about asking unfamiliar people for assistance.

This requires you to dig deep into your courage reserves. It's another act of positive rebellion to create support for yourself when it feels like it's not there, since you're rejecting any notions that you are powerless. Try not to give up. Eventually, support will appear, even if you have to build it yourself from scratch. By taking charge in this case of having to meet your own needs, you will show the universe that you are taking care of you. You will attract like-minded souls who are here to assist you with your journey.

Even if you're really busy, it's still possible to create systems of support for yourself online, using e-mail or private groups on social-media websites. It can feel comforting to have a sacred space set aside, dedicated to receiving support and unconditional love, especially if you're stirring things up in the rest of your life.

Exercise: Are Your Needs Being Met?

1. In your journal, list all of your needs, both personal and professional.

2. Place a check mark by each personal need that is being met. You might be surprised to see that you're able to check off quite a few items.

3. Next to each unmet need, write down what would help you the most in the way of helpful people, resources, loving support, and any other tools. Notice if you have some of these right now and are just not utilizing them. If you don't ask for a hand, you might be depriving others of the joy of being of service.

4. Write down what would help you feel like you can rock the boat and make the necessary changes.

When you do this exercise, you may realize that you would like assistance in many areas. Perhaps you need technological support for figuring out some new software. Or you might discover that you need to take some classes to increase your knowledge in some way. Other needs could be anything from receiving a monthly massage to having someone cook dinner for you now and then to having a regular girls' night out to relax with your friends. So let's address anything currently not being taken care of.

Exercise: Action Plan to Get Your Needs Met

Don't worry if there seem to be a lot of unchecked items on the list you just made. If you don't want to take action right now, you can return to this exercise later. The following steps will simply help you see that you do have choices:

1. Look at the unchecked items from your list and circle the three that are the most pressing.

2. On a new journal page or a separate piece of paper, write down the items you chose and review what you wrote about what would help you most. Under each one, list three to five small action steps you can take in order to get the need met. Don't stop yourself from including things that seem off limits, unrealistic, or expensive—things that might rock the boat. Write them down anyway.

3. Circle one action step for each unmet need, choosing the one that feels best for you.

4. Work on one unmet need per week for the next three weeks, using the circled action step as your homework.

If you feel that you might get stuck in doing this exercise, be sure to find someone you can be accountable to, such as a close friend that you check in with at the end of each week. It's also okay if your action plan changes. Your needs may evolve, so be sure to reevaluate your needs and adjust your plan from time to time. I recommend checking in with yourself monthly.

Riding the Waves

Rocking the boat is risky. And if it's difficult in your personal life, the stakes can be even higher at work, where your livelihood is on the line. I've witnessed some women apologizing for being talented or powerful in the workplace, instead of seeking promotions. I've heard stories of professional women trying to do everything on their own, worrying that asking for help will be seen as a sign of weakness. I've also given countless readings to women who would like to break out of the traditional working world, running their own businesses or at least using flextime or telecommuting.

Going for the security instead of following your passion and purpose is a normal human response. Although I encourage you to rock the boat and live your truth, I don't usually advocate just up and quitting your day job. Rather, I propose the idea of starting your own thing on the side while you have the stability to reliably pay your bills. It's very stressful and soul stretching to not have your basic needs met as you're trying to take care of your business, which can be as taxing as caring for a new baby.

Of course, some people make dramatic professional and financial choices and do just fine. But many times they had the mind-set in place that helped them to be a success, perhaps having enjoyed success in a similar life area, so there was evidence that they could make it happen with their businesses.

Does the thought of mixing it up at work make you freeze? Or do you blaze trails on the job but dread rocking the boat socially? Rebel chick mystics come at these challenges from different angles, so it can be helpful to think about how you feel about taking risks in many different life areas. When you listed your needs and checked off the personal needs that had been met, did you notice that most of what remained unchecked was professional? Return to that list and repeat the exercises you completed for personal needs with the work-related items you wrote down. As you address those needs, you'll move toward creating more balance in your life—even as you continue making waves!

If you feel still feel stuck, though, try not to wait for others to give you permission to take actions that your heart calls you to take. When you embark upon something new, it might be tempting to go into research mode, going online and asking for as many opinions as possible before you make a decision. Or you might procrastinate as long as possible, until you're practically forced to make changes by life circumstances. Try to avoid freaking out or engaging in self-defeating thoughts and unhealthy behaviors. Start to think about whether your approach to making changes truly serves you. Life doesn't have to be so difficult. After weathering the storms, you might even decide to ride the waves, propelling yourself to your destination.

By now, you may have already made the decision to make things easier, since you've done so much work on having your needs met. In the next chapter, you'll learn more about leaving those tough times behind you.

Chapter Six

Drop Out of the School of Hard Knocks

*"Meanwhile, life keeps moving forward.
The truth is, there's no better time to be
happy than right now. If not now, when?"*

— RICHARD CARLSON

Another form of positive rebellion is to let go of the idea that life has to be difficult. Our time on this planet is often likened to a classroom in spiritual literature. Just as you get to select which college you attend, you get to choose your school for learning life lessons. Some women opt for the School of Hard Knocks, believing that personal growth and healing are part of an arduous path. They also might think that it takes a long time to become happy, healthy, or successful, or that they have to work to earn good things.

The School of Hard Knocks can involve tears, lost hope, lack of self-confidence, fears about moving forward, worries about what others will think, losing sight of goals and dreams, illness, financial hardship, and conflict. Sometimes enrolling in this program is unintentional. You might not have thought of attending classes elsewhere, such as the School of Joy, or any other name that feels right for you.

Enrolling in a more enjoyable program just requires an intention to start learning lessons in easier ways, ones that feel better—you can use your own words to describe your intention. You get to start choosing which classes you'd like to take, similar to starting college and selecting your major. Rebel chick mystics are on a modern path, so some of the courses tend to be related to contemporary challenges. Of course, most traditional institutions have requirements, but when it comes to life school, I invite you to pick your own required courses. Perhaps you've already taken classes such as Heartbreak 101 or the graduate track, Heartbreak 401? Have you completed Bankruptcy 401 or Divorce 101? Perhaps you're ready for a new schedule filled with Relaxing More 101, Enjoying My Job 401, Being Happy 501, or Feeling Peaceful 601.

You get to choose when you drop the painful course work. When you do, it doesn't mean that you're done learning; it means that you're ready to move on to a more joyful curriculum. I encourage you to read this chapter with the intention of releasing yourself from the School of Hard Knocks.

It's Okay to Be Happy

Choosing to be happy is a powerful form of positive rebellion. When you make this decision, it can feel like you're straying from the herd by rejecting the mass consciousness. If you regularly participate in consuming popular media, it can seem that much of the world is unhappy, filled with violence, crime, hate, wars, natural disasters, economic distress, materialism, and pollution. Advertising can make you feel as though you need material things, including many technical gadgets or even pharmaceuticals, to be happy.

Some popular reality television shows depict people undergoing massive transformation, but much of it is external, more of a focus on appearance. As a result, you might feel that you need to alter yourself substantially. Some recent studies, including one by the University of Pennsylvania in 2009, show that women's happiness has declined, especially relative to men's, despite women's well-being improving in many areas such as career during the past few decades.

All of the negative aspects of modern life might make you stop to wonder if you are or can really be happy. I encourage you to embrace life on your own terms. Marianne Williamson said it best in her book *A Woman's Worth:* "The world is terrified of joyful women. Make a stand. Be one anyway." Part of you might even feel guilty for choosing to live in a more joyful way when you see others struggling or being unhappy. I encourage you to rebel against this tendency to feel guilty, too. Others have their own classes that they've elected to take. They have to be the ones to switch schools. The most helpful thing that you can do is to lead by example. You may inspire them (when they are ready) to drop out of the School of Hard Knocks as well.

Shifting your intention to learn and grow in easier ways could seem difficult, especially if you grew up with any authority figures who believed that life was hard. As a child, I was surrounded by hard-working, blue-collar factory workers, and I think this made me believe that a lot of effort was necessary, not only to earn a living, but also to be happy. I internalized the idea that you needed to work first, and then you could have fun later.

Some rebel chick mystics have described how conflicted they felt about their family of origin's religious beliefs, especially the idea that they needed to atone for their sins by doing hard personal work through prayers, acts of love, or acts of deprivation. Some of them internalized the idea that happiness would only come when they arrived in heaven, after spending their entire lives working diligently to perfect themselves.

If you inherited ideas like this, you might be tempted to push yourself to receive a top score in your life classes. Previously, I mentioned that high achievers may be drawn to spiritual disciplines; they may also choose to take their lessons very seriously. I just want to give you another gentle reminder that you can choose the level of personal work and the type of spiritual path you follow. As I emphasize in each chapter, you don't have to do all the exercises in this book. You can only change or heal your own life, and your lessons will be different from another's. If you focus on doing what makes you happy, challenges may not seem so difficult. When you feel better, you can respond in loving or peaceful ways to challenging people and situations.

Even if you choose, say, the School of Joy, you still may encounter challenges from time to time. If you've been working on your growth for a while, you might wonder if there is any end in sight. You could have spent a lot of time, effort, or even money on healing during your years attending the School of Hard Knocks. You may have searched for the perfect textbook that made sense in helping you deal with the obstacles you faced.

Some of my clients have expressed that they felt impatient at times, wondering when their lives would improve once and for all. Some of them made a decision to put their foot down, refusing to recycle old patterns any longer. Others sometimes wrote to me in despair, with e-mail subject lines such as, "Not this again!" or "I thought that I was done with this!" I can relate, since I also experienced a seemingly repetitive pattern of negative life lessons.

I know I say this a lot, but it's important: *Healing is a process.* It might seem as though patterns persist for a while. One way to look at this is that the lessons themselves are not repeating, but rather that there are many layers that need to be healed. It's not that you've enrolled in a remedial course in the School of Hard Knocks when these other layers appear. It's more like receiving a new module that comes with an answer key in your life classes. You get a bit of new information, but since you've had a similar challenge before, you're better prepared. You've attained some wisdom and grace from your past experiences of being able to turn things around. When these layers come up, you can still let yourself be happy underneath it all.

How to Choose to Be Happy

You might be wondering how you can choose to be happy. Not allowing the chaos in the world to affect you is one thing, but what about when you're feeling surrounded by many negative, unhappy people who have symptoms of *crapitude,* or negative outlook? There's a positive way to think about those negative types: They are simply showing you how you don't want to be, reminding you that you don't wish to attend classes at the School of Hard Knocks.

According to some spiritual teachers, others in our lives mirror us, including the aspects of ourselves that we've not learned to love as of yet.

In any case, there are still challenges. One simple way to manage negativity is to make a daily, conscious effort to behave and choose differently from those unpleasant people (or the part of you that's unpleasant, too). Once again, you're engaged in positive rebellion.

Here's a list of some negative things that some unhappy people tend to say to help you recognize what you want to rebel against in the future:

- *I feel like a victim of life circumstances.*
- *I feel like my life is so difficult. Poor me.*
- *I feel lost.*
- *I feel frustrated.*
- *I feel stuck.*
- *I never have any fun.*
- *I think my problems are due to other people.*
- *I don't think my life will ever get better.*
- *I am angry at life.*
- *I feel ready to give up.*
- *I don't feel like being loving because no one else is.*

No worries, by the way, if you've ever been able to identify with some of those statements. (But if you've felt like that for a prolonged time, you may be depressed. If so, it might be good to receive some help from a physician or counselor.)

Your rebellion can come internally, when you refuse to believe these ideas for yourself or others. When you hear or read sentiments like these, you can tell yourself some-thing like, *That might be true for that person, but it doesn't have to be true for me. I prefer to be happy. I know that I can take charge to change my life.* Or you can lighten up by re-peating the negative statements aloud in a whiny or dron-ing voice, similar to the character Debbie Downer from *Saturday Night Live.* Whether it comes from within you or from others, humor is an excellent method for breaking up old perspectives.

When you start to choose happiness, you will notice that your relationships begin to shift. As you feel and act more positively, others may be less likely to tell you their same tales of woe repeatedly. You might find your-self not joining in to tell your similar stories of unhappi-ness. Instead of living the saying, "Misery loves company," you might find yourself living according to the idea that "Company hates misery," meaning positive people tend to not want to surround themselves with the crapitude.

Exercise: Rewriting Your Story

Another act of positive rebellion—and a great way to choose happiness—is to rewrite your life story, since the aspects that feel limiting or negative might be prevent-ing you from being as happy as you would like. I did it myself, using the exercise that follows, which is modified from one that a life coach gave me years ago. I had a big a-ha moment, realizing that I'd been treating my personal healing path like a part-time job added to my already-busy schedule. I learned to ease up on myself, focusing more on fun and self-care such as receiving massages, taking naps, and enjoying my hobbies, instead of racing around to so many appointments each week. My desire is that you achieve your own epiphanies from this work.

You are the author of your own life story. It's up to you to determine the plot and the characters. If you repeatedly tell others a negative story about your life lessons, it can keep you stuck in the past. Perhaps we tell the same tales over and over because we want someone to witness our pain, or maybe we're seeking validation, or simply someone to listen to us. The past is not easy to deal with at times, but there will be moments that you may feel a gentle wake-up call to start letting go of its hold on you.

Part of the law of attraction is that you draw in what you think about the most. The words you speak about your life come from your habitual ways of thinking. Words are very powerful, since they can create your experiences. This exercise can help you start revising your thinking and the words that you use to describe the future. As you write, think of your journal like a trusted friend and confidant who will really listen to you. (If you're not ready to delve into your life story, however, it's okay to skip this exercise altogether or return to it later.)

1. In your journal, write down your life story in whatever detail you desire. You don't have to write chronologically. Take your time. You might decide to return to the painful parts later on if they become too emotionally challenging for you.

2. When you feel ready, look for the recurring themes. Write them down, using emotional ideas for categorization, such as: heartbreak, doubt, faith, friendship, relationships, life purpose, challenges, happiness, freedom, education, feeling tested, letting go, and finding myself.

3. After looking at the recurring themes, write a new story about your life. As you rewrite, you can reframe hardships, detailing the positive lessons that you've learned along the way. For example, maybe you've gained qualities such as patience, compassion, or tolerance for others or yourself. You can detail how your challenges have made you into the wise, loving person that you are today. It's also possible that you'll want to completely reject certain themes. If you want, you can go back and write about how you would've handled things in the past if you had the knowledge and wisdom that you do today.

4. Detail the reality that you'd like to create for yourself. Looking at your past patterns helps you get clear about what you'd like to build in the future. You might want to have one new experience or outlook, or you may want to create an entirely brand-new life. You get to create what feels right for you. Pretend that you've been transported to the future you'd like to live in. Write down all of the juicy, fun details.

5. After you rewrite your life story, replacing the old narrative with the new one, read over your work. You might feel so good that you decide to destroy or toss your old narrative. It's up to you.

If you decide not to destroy your old life story, you can use it as a gut check. When life feels really overwhelming or challenging, you can reread your account of the past to gain perspective. It can remind you of how far you've come on your path. Then you can reread your new story to bolster your hope and positive belief in yourself, along with a reminder that you can rewrite even the current chapter of your life if it's not making you happy. This is great preparation for your exit from the School of Hard Knocks.

It's also useful to think about how you learned your lessons. What's your style for creating transformation? Are you gentle, steady, and slow, or are you more abrupt or intense? Some women completely deconstruct their lives to make a new start. I've witnessed many types of transformations, and I consider all of them to be undertaken by brave souls. I've heard some women try to diminish their courage by saying that their actions were "nothing," compared to seemingly stronger women they've known. I see all changes as big, from rejecting popular ideas to asserting your needs to packing up to move cross-country.

You can find inspiration in many forms. If you feel alone in your new story, you can look at how other women have rewritten theirs by choosing to turn around their obstacles. A couple of books that you might want to check out are *The Diary of a Young Girl* by Anne Frank and *Left to Tell* by Immaculée Ilibagiza.

On a very different note, it's fun to read or listen to female humorists such as Loretta LaRoche, who helps women take life less seriously. You can also turn to the healing powers of music. Listen to some inspirational songs about overcoming difficulties from your personal music collection.

Quiz: Are You Ready to Rock Out to a Different Tune?

When you get tired of hearing yourself tell your old story from the School of Hard Knocks, try using humor to shake it up. Maybe besides telling a new story, you also need to sing a new song. The following are partial and sometimes silly song lyrics that I made up for this purpose. Pick the one that best fits the old story you've been telling; the answer key will reveal which genre it fits into. For extra credit, complete the lyrics! You might also research songs by artists in the genre you selected for more understanding and laughs.

1. *I've had so much trouble in my life. I've cried myself to sleep. My eyes feel like the sky, raining tears from up high. No one understands, so I think I'll be alone since it's easier that way. I don't have anywhere that feels like home.*

2. *My dog died. I lost my happy home. I was fired from my job. My spouse left me. My truck broke down. I'm stuck in the mud.*

3. *I fall in love, and I always get hurt. This only seems to happen to me. I am home alone on most Saturday nights. I wonder why this only happens to me. I feel lovesick.*

4. *Life sucks. The world is messed up. Governments lie. Corporations suck. Screw authority. I can't be the real me since people don't understand me.*

5. *I hate myself, and sometimes I don't want to live on this planet. Everyone I've ever loved has left me. My parents were never around. What's the point? I think I'll stay in bed today. I'm too sensitive to live in this world.*

6. *It's time to party. My life makes more sense when I'm having fun and in love. I party to avoid my problems.*

7. *Life makes me angry. I feel like screaming. I'm so intense, but it's better that way. No one tells me what to do.*

8. *Life isn't easy. Society holds me back. It's hard to stay on your feet. It's hard to live in these streets.*

Answer key:

1. The blues
2. Country
3. Pop ballad
4. Punk rock
5. Emo
6. Rock and roll
7. Heavy metal
8. Hip hop

When you catch yourself telling the same story, review your song selection. It will help you lighten up a bit.

You can write a new song, too, if you feel ready. You might even change lyrics to songs you like to be more positive. For example, a friend of mine sang Gloria Gaynor's song "I Will Survive" as "I Will Thrive" instead, altering some of the lyrics besides the chorus as well. You also can use your Sassy, Confident Theme song from Chapter 4, instead of rewriting existing numbers.

Know that all of the songs from the quiz, regardless of genre, can be written in a more positive way. Of course, at times you'll feel like listening to the originals to process, cleanse, and release. Just try not to dwell in the negative energies for too long. I don't buy into the idea of music being good or bad. Rather, it's another healing tool in your life.

Exercise: Rock Your Courage, Strength, and Wisdom

Even though your old story might feel depressing or challenging, or cause you pain or even shame, it made you the person that you are today. It was perfect for your journey. Sometimes it helps us to see that some of our challenges were in our lives for a purpose.

I've heard some rebel chick mystics ask, "Why did I have to go through all of that hard stuff?" There's no exact or one-size-fits-all answer to that question. It might just be that it will make more sense later. Perhaps you needed a certain situation so that you could help others with similar challenges in the future.

This exercise will help you start to make sense of your time attending the School of Hard Knocks, so get out your journal and complete the following statements:

1. *When I look at my own life story, I feel so proud of myself because . . .*

2. *The biggest blessings from experiencing my challenges are . . .*

3. *The most important things I've learned about myself are . . .*

4. *I learned that my strengths are . . .*

5. *My challenges have given me wisdom. The wisdom that I want to share with others is . . .*

6. *The following positive adjectives best describe my true self . . .*

7. *I'm the hero in my own life story because . . .*

8. *The skills and talents I've acquired through my challenges are . . .*

9. *People would be amazed to know that I'm . . .*

10. My challenges have prepared me for the next chapter of my life in these ways . . .

As you read what you wrote, really allow yourself to bask in the positive energy. Let yourself see what an amazing woman you are. You rock! You have gained courage, strength, and wisdom. Embrace all of the good that has arisen from any heartache, despair, or other challenges. You might wish at this point to see if you are ready to fully let go of the hard lessons, dropping out of the School of Hard Knocks.

It's okay if you don't feel ready, especially if you are grieving, working through crisis, experiencing major life change, or getting over severe disappointments or setbacks. In those cases, please be gentle with yourself, trying to trust that you're exactly where you need to be in your healing journey. Let yourself experience the full range of your emotions, getting support where needed, and complete this chapter at another time

If you are ready to move on, proceed with the final sections of this chapter.

Dropping Out

By now, I hope you see that you're an expert in getting through challenges. You could probably write a book about how you made it through life in one piece. If you're reading this, you most likely are ready to see the last of the School of Hard Knocks!

Although we might all be qualified to earn Ph.D.'s from the School of Hard Knocks, it's empowering to know that we don't have to stick it out in that grueling place anymore. As you mentally see yourself walking out the door of that school, never to return, know that you can award yourself your own degree on your own terms. Feel free to have a small party for yourself—this is especially fun with fellow rebels! This can be a wonderful time. It's also time to plan for your future.

Exercise: Exit Interview

As you leave the School of Hard Knocks, I have some additional questions for you. Think of me as similar to your academic advisor, but a loving one who is going to cheer you on by saying, "You rock!" In your journal, write down the answers to the following questions. Be as honest as you can.

1. Which teachers do you want to thank the most? (Consider actual teachers, mentors, friends, relatives, loved ones, diseases, and challenges.)

2. Which classes were the hardest? Which ones did you enjoy the most?

3. How will you continue to learn and grow?

4. When you find yourself telling your old story—hanging out on the old school grounds—what strategies and action plan will you use to shift into a more positive place?

5. What advice would you give to other women who are still going to those painful classes?

6. Which new school are you going to pick, instead of the School of Hard Knocks, to continue your personal growth and spiritual path? (Give it a name, such as School of Joy, as I suggested, or one that speaks to your spirit.)

Congratulations on your liberation! I hope you feel ready to rock the world even more. Try not to feel overwhelmed or as though you have to be perfect to move forward. It's okay to be a work in progress.

Healing your old life story doesn't have to be expensive, time-consuming, or difficult. Perhaps you've experienced profound healing from seeing a sunset or receiving a hug at just the right moment, or from hearing loving words at the right moment. It's also okay to get some help, which is what the next chapter is about.

Chapter Seven

Don't Do-It-Yourself

"For fast-acting relief, try slowing down."

— LILY TOMLIN

So many women try to be a superwoman. They think that by doing everything on their own, they become their most powerful selves. As we explored in Chapter 2, it's tempting to strive for perfection and take the concept of do-it-yourself a bit too far at times.

Do-it-yourself (DIY) became a popular term in the 1950s, describing a way to avoid hiring experts in order to save money on home-improvement projects. The phrase has since extended to refer to other areas, such as crafting and music, and I apply it more broadly yet in discussing life balance.

DIY is popular with unconventional types since it's sometimes seen as the ultimate rebellion against the authority figures or experts that you traditionally had to consult or employ to get things done. For rebel chick mystics, however, admitting, "I need some help," is a simple act of positive rebellion. You're rejecting the notions that women have to be everything to everyone, have to get tasks at home and work done on their own, and have to figure out new skill sets alone. Instead, you're choosing to ask for help, a path that isn't always well-traveled.

This chapter will ask you to take additional steps around the familiar topic of receiving help, letting go of any remaining perfectionism that could be lingering. The importance of getting support is emphasized so much in this book since for many women, it can be so difficult to shift into receiving mode after years of not asking for help. This starts at such a young age. In recent years, the non-profit organization Girls, Incorporated, has done extensive research through Harris Interactive on the pressure felt by modern girls. Their survey "The Supergirl Dilemma: Girls Grapple with the Mounting Pressure of Expectations" features girls giving their honest opinions about how they feel the need to be successful, thin, accommodating, and perfect.

Since the very young are feeling so many pressures, it follows that adults might have some work to do on letting go of their DIY superwoman tendencies. You also may need to learn how to delegate tasks, receive more help or emotional support, and let go of the strong need to fly solo.

In *Women's Bodies, Women's Wisdom*, Christiane Northrup, M.D., talks about her journey to release the idea that if she wanted things done correctly, then she had to do them herself. She created a support system for herself at home and at work, calling it "assisted living." Later in this chapter, we'll look at ways you can create even more support for yourself, especially helping you figure out how to get involved in groups, which are very important.

Overturning the DIY Lie

DIY sometimes is a great way to feel empowered. It works well for making cupcakes, sewing baby clothing, making your band's demo, and redoing your patio. In other areas, it doesn't end up serving you well. Women often feel that they have to do everything themselves simply because they know they are capable of it. This mind-set can create a high level of stress, as women try to be experts in everything. I believe that you really end up shortchanging your spirit, along with possibly exhausting yourself, if you attempt to constantly DIY.

The thing is, you can't know everything, and you can't do it all on your own. This is why *DIY is a lie.* Even experts hire assistants and subject-matter experts from time to time. Understand that there are some positive aspects of asking for help:

1. You give someone else the satisfaction from being of service.

2. You help others earn a living doing what they enjoy, by paying for their expertise.

3. You free up some of your time so that you can focus on other areas and even get more rest.

4. You demonstrate to the universe that you're willing to be helped. This can open you up to receiving more good.

5. You might learn new things that you'll be able to use later in some way. When you hire experts, you can pick up tips, tricks, or guidance as you consult with them.

6. You can reduce stress, freeing up the energy
   that is being used to worry so that you can
   work on other aspects of projects and your life.

If the idea of asking for help still challenges you, take out your journal and write down your own reasons why it's positive to get some relief when you're feeling overwhelmed, tired, or overextended. This list can be a good reminder later if feelings of guilt or stress start to creep into your mind.

You may need to flex some courage muscles to rebel against the lie that you can do it all yourself. You could have been conditioned to believe that household duties like cooking and cleaning are your job. If you aren't the breadwinner, you may be pressuring yourself to do all of the child care and household management. My female coaching clients who telecommute mention that it's hard to ignore the piles of dirty laundry or dishes, so they take care of them, just because it seems easier than asking others to help out. I've also heard women say that they feel guilty watching a loved one do something they feel they could have done. Maybe you've had similar thoughts as you watch your spouse or children do chores that you assigned, also telling yourself that in the time it took to tell them what to do, you could have taken care of it yourself. Sometimes women are comfortable asking for help, but not *receiving* it.

Besides asking for (and receiving) help at work and at home, it's okay to get support with the healing process. Even though the industry is called "self-help," it doesn't mean you have to do it all alone. Although I emphasize that you know what's best for yourself, I think it's possible to take the natural-medicine idea that you're your own best healer a bit too far.

It's great to have tools such as journaling, affirmations, meditation, natural remedies, books, and classes when you have physical, mental, emotional, or spiritual challenges. But make sure this doesn't prevent you from seeing and using other methods that could help you. If pain of any kind or illness becomes unbearable, you might need to hire the appropriate professional, who may even be a traditional medical doctor.

In the past, I thought that I could figure out any physical challenge since I had reversed very trying health conditions, including chronic fatigue syndrome, on my own. On a few memorable occasions, my physical body begged to differ, being in intense pain. This may seem extreme, but please be aware that the DIY lie can be powerful, especially for rebel chick mystics. The lesson is that you can't always be your own healer, doctor, counselor, life coach, dentist, or massage therapist.

It's possible that you actually may end up saving money and time by hiring help for your pressing challenges, since sometimes an expert can find shortcuts. There also may be free or low-cost options, such as low-cost beauty services at cosmetology schools or free or donation-based psychological counseling by graduate students at local universities. I've seen reduced-fee massage therapy and discounted child care, group coaching, and yoga classes; often, there are free support groups for various situations. The Internet can be used to find bartering groups when it comes to services that you might need for your home, business, or healing. The universe has much help available. There are pleasant surprises waiting for you.

Trying to be a DIY superwoman will tire you out. But if you enjoy doing certain things, keep on doing them. If other responsibilities cause you stress or make you tired, it's time to start making changes in your daily life. The following exercise will help you clarify things, along with starting to make a plan for obtaining help.

Exercise: Prioritizing Your Daily Life

In *The Passion Test,* Janet Attwood and Chris Attwood mention the importance of having a visible list of your passions. When I work with clients, I prefer that they start out with having a list of priorities. I believe that this will make it easier to find some time for their passions. If you are a DIY superwoman, following your dreams might be the last thing on your mind—or perhaps you're pursuing them intensely, without rest and recovery.

I'm having you start out by identifying your priorities, because if you know what's important, you can make more informed decisions about how you spend your time. You may want to refer to the work you did in Chapter 1 on prioritizing your roles, since this exercise takes it one step further. Now let's get started:

1. In your journal, make a list of all of your unique skills, talents, and abilities that are related to daily life. Write them all down, including the ones that seem mundane or required. No one else does things with the same style as you. If you make the most delicious, healthy meals, put that down. If you're a great listener to your co-workers, be sure to include that, too. Maybe you write entertaining blog posts, or you give amazing bear hugs. Really take some time with your list and get it all down.

2. Once you feel you've completely captured your skills, go back and circle or star the ones that you enjoy doing the most. Pick your top five or ten items.

3. I invite you to make these items the focal point of your life. What you do the best and enjoy the most is meant to be your priority. You will still get to the other items most likely, but your energy and focus will be more on what you love.

4. Write your top priorities from Step 3 on a note card, and carry it in your purse or pocket. Looking at it from time to time throughout your day will remind you of living according to what's important to you.

I also highly recommend that you check out the process outlined in *The Passion Test*. It will help you get clear on the top five passions that set your soul on fire. You might also use the same method as you did with your priorities, writing down all of the things that you're passionate about and then picking the top five. Or if you already know those things, write them down on the same page as your priority list in your journal, as well as on the note card that you'll carry with you.

Joining Forces

One of the stereotypes about traditional rebels is that they are loners. The DIY mind-set, as you know, can be popular with unconventional types. But belonging to groups, instead of going it alone, can be another form of positive rebellion. Since our society is competitive, the idea of teamwork might get lost unless it is taught or fostered. In addition, women sometimes feel especially uncomfortable about being in groups. You may have experienced communication difficulties, whether socially or professionally, along with the pressure to be "better"—thinner, prettier, smarter, or more accomplished.

I always cringed when I noticed any catty comments or negative energy directed at me by other women. After experiencing the good feelings from teamwork in sports, it felt so strange to encounter that negativity in work or social settings. It turns out that my instincts were correct, however, and that groups are good for us. If you study successful people, you'll notice that they form partnerships with others, such as working together through joint ventures.

Rebellious types sometimes worry about losing their freedom, and the DIY superwoman mind-set often is, "I want to do it *my* way!" Yet if you hang out in groups, you can get new ideas and insights or moral support for a project you're working on, a decision you're making, or something you're healing in your life. Another blessing is that you can share things you enjoy with other women, doing these activities together. You might want to start a book club, a social club, a gardening club, a support group for stay-at-home moms, a business-networking group, or anything that makes your heart sing. I've seen clubs of all kinds for women, even a daredevil one—where members gathered each month to learn how to skydive, eat fire, and tame lions!

Many of my clients are writers, musicians, artists, stay-at-home moms, freelancers in different fields, or telecommuters. They enjoy aspects of being at home, but many say that they need balance, requiring some time with other women for support, ideas, and companionship as part of their personal self-care programs. Since you're a modern mystic, you may enjoy spending time with others for activities such as meditation, yoga, discussion of spiritual books, or healing. It can feel good to connect with other souls on a similar journey, getting out of your hermit's cave. It's another option for support and to help you enjoy your path more.

Even if you tend to prefer your own company most of the time, it can be enjoyable and sustain your spirit to spend time in groups every now and then. If you're already comfortable with the idea of groups, this is great. You most likely have received some benefits or value from interacting with others in the past.

If resistance comes up for you, this is okay. It can feel scary to put yourself out there, especially if you grew up feeling as though you didn't fit in. You might not fully trust groups. If you're nervous, try to honor yourself. You might be more comfortable in smaller gatherings such as with one or two friends. This more limited interaction still counts! You can also dabble, trying out various groups that appeal to you, to see where you want to focus your time. As you venture out, you will push the edges of your comfort zone. You may also choose to belong to an online group, instead of an in-person one.

All of this is okay, but don't miss out on the wonderful things life has to offer you, including the people who can support you on your path. Watch any of your tendencies to feel as though you need to figure out everything on your own. They're subtle signs of being a DIY superwoman. Warning signs include feeling as though you're going to burden others or that it's easier to be alone.

Life is not meant to be a struggle. When you feel supported, it's easier to step outside your comfort zone, as one of many benefits. When you're in a group situation that you enjoy, you can be reminded of who you are apart from all your roles, including wife, mother, employee, sister, daughter, and friend. It can feel reassuring to have some women in your life who are interested you as a person, including your goals and dreams.

When you step into a different environment, you'll be able to see the bigger picture of who you are. You'll find that others have similar experiences, which can be helpful to yours. When a fellow group member has a big dream that resembles yours, you won't feel so alone in moving forward to pursue it since you're in good company. It can feel like opening a forgotten treasure chest when you're reminded of old goals that were on the back burner.

You'll love seeing the law of attraction in action in groups. You could find that you have many things in common with the women you meet, enjoying how the divine has brought you together for some purpose, whether it's for friendship, support, or working on professional goals.

Speaking of purpose, I've found it very beneficial to be in groups with women when it comes to support for my life purpose. Sometimes our loved ones aren't always able to support us in the ways that we want or that feel best for us. Even if you have family members and old friends on your side, it's still useful to have others as your cheerleaders, giving you ideas and guidance.

The rebel chick mystics I've worked with report that life purpose is one of their most pressing concerns. In the past, you may have worked with career counselors, read books, and taken assessments, but still not feel any closer to figuring it out. Or you might know a basic aspect of your life purpose, but not be sure which steps to take next. Sometimes your purpose is multifaceted, not just one thing or one area, but there's no reason to stress out if you're not sure, because the next chapter is about how to find your life purpose.

Chapter Eight

Find Your Life Purpose

"Do not go where the path may lead, go instead where there is no path and leave a trail."

— RALPH WALDO EMERSON

It can seem daunting to find your purpose. There are so many ideas and so much information to sift through. Some spiritual teachers say that your purpose is to simply be happy, others believe that it's to be of service to others. Even I bring you additional ideas.

As a teacher, I tend to differentiate job, career, calling, and life purpose. Sometimes these areas intersect, sometimes they don't. I define *job* as a position you work in that lets you earn a living. A *career* is an area of work, a field, or a path in which you've chosen to find a job. Your *calling* and *life purpose* are very similar, although I tend to see calling as the spiritual side. In giving psychic readings to many women, I've heard simple phrases to describe a calling, such as "to love," "to serve," "to bring more joy and laughter into the world," "to usher in world peace," and "to help humanity become more prosperous."

Intuitive animal communicator Cindie Davis uses the term *baseline* when discussing her calling. She believes that her baseline is the divine spark that aids her faith in remembering her dreams and goals, saying, "When others tell me I can't, that is when I reach for the stars, whispering that I can."

You might be wondering if you can achieve your goals. It's possible that you're tired from working hard in the past to find your life purpose. You may have tried out various career paths or programs of study in attempts to find that *one thing* that will make your heart sing. (But as you will see, your life purpose may be a combination of things.) You may have read numerous books or even taken expensive tests to help you gain clarity around which career would suit you the best.

I took one of those tests in the past, and it revealed that my best career would be as a musician! This stressed me out a great deal since I was going through the dark night of the soul, and I was considering abandoning my dreams in order to return to the conventional work force and become more of a breadwinner in my household. Today, I understand more about how that test result revealed much about my calling as a musician. The experience invited me to look deeper within, discovering that it was okay to have more than one aspect to my life purpose. (Later, I'll discuss the idea of a multifaceted life purpose in more depth.)

Maybe you have talked to a good number of people such as career counselors, life coaches, healers, or psychics to work on gaining clarity. At times, you may have been mainly concerned with earning a living, just as I was. Or you might have been too exhausted to think about whether you're following your true path.

I encourage all rebel chick mystics to consider the concept of life purpose in simple, empowered ways to help alleviate and transform some of the possibly overwhelming feelings and concerns. Life purpose is the path that you choose for yourself. In the movie *The Secret,* Neale Donald Walsch explains this idea in a vivid way. He says that there is no place in the universe with a blackboard that lists your name along with a definition of exactly what your purpose is. Only you know what it might be, and only you can live it.

Some women worry that they're not on track, and many desire to not only earn a living, but to leave behind a positive legacy. Maybe you're also searching for the perfect job while wondering if your choices will make a difference in the world. Try to consider that you *are* having an impact, even if it's in a small way. All contributions are important and needed.

Paving Your Own Way

Even if you're clear on what your life purpose is, many old ideas may have been holding you back. You might have felt pressure for external achievements such as title or salary while neglecting your happiness or well-being. Even if you're an adult, your parents could be influencing your plans in a subtle way, since there may still be a part of you that wants to please them.

I asked my friend and colleague Lea Whitefeather, a talented makeup artist and metaphysical practitioner, to share how she overcame these pressures. Her story may help you to work on shifting any limiting ideas you have absorbed, so that you too can pave your own way when it comes to life purpose.

Lea's Story

Since I was a little girl, I've questioned why we can't simply live our dreams. I grew up around authority figures whose ideas of life were more conventional than my own, so I was frequently encouraged to be a doctor or a lawyer, rather than the artist I am at heart. I also encountered many of their doubts and fears regarding my spiritual and metaphysical curiosities since I was surrounded by traditionally religious people.

Nevertheless, beginning in my teens, I fervently studied subjects such as Reiki, astrology, reincarnation, hypnosis, and intuition, both formally and informally. Following my heart eventually led me to live a happy, prosperous life. I followed a blessed string of synchronicities that I wouldn't have been open to had I acted out of a need to please others, instead of listening to my personal truth.

Along the way, I've experienced several challenges, including being temporarily homeless, living out of a van with my fiancé and our two dogs. But I feel enriched, empowered, and fulfilled because I've learned my life lessons on my own terms. I've grown because I didn't walk down roads simply because they were already paved. I actually went the way that called out to me, giving my life more meaning than I know it would have if I lived somebody else's dream.

Today, I am a makeup artist working as both a freelancer and with a major cosmetics company. It amazes me to see where I am now, since when I was younger, many discouraged me from majoring in art history because they didn't see the value in becoming an artist or thought it wouldn't be easy to get work in art-related fields. With help from the Universe and with the support of like-minded souls, I'd certainly say that life's working out more than just all right.

Lea's story shows that it's possible to pave your own road, even if those around you don't initially feel supportive. Some women have multiple talents and interests, all of which can be part of their purpose.

You may not always fit into a traditional corporate environment, so you might create other working arrangements such as self-employment, consulting, or working multiple part-time jobs—or some combination of these options.

According to recent studies, there are more and more female entrepreneurs these days. My mentor and friend Gail Trauco exemplifies this. Gail is a nurse and a highly successful entrepreneur, owning a million-dollar business doing what she loves: working on clinical trials in oncology and surgical and critical care. She triumphed over many challenges, including childhood poverty and being a single mom raising three sons while overcoming two difficult divorces, obesity, and losing her prior clinical research company.

Along the way, Gail added psychic medium, hypnotherapist, and healer to her skill set. She bravely puts all aspects of her life purpose out into the world with no apologies. I share her story as a reminder that you can do whatever your heart desires. You have many options for a successful path, even if you face serious obstacles. If you're interested in creating an independent option, do some research and see what you find. I highly recommend

A Rebel Chick Mystic's Guide

Kimberly Wilson's book *Tranquilista* (which I also mentioned in Chapter 1) for resources for female entrepreneurs.

If the idea of being self-employed scares you a little bit, that's okay. You still can serve your purpose at a traditional day job, if that feels better to you. Or you can arrange everything so that working independently is a good fit. Taking it one step at a time can be less stressful than abruptly handing in your resignation. Keep on taking small steps toward your life purpose, using the tools you'll develop in this chapter, because things get clearer as you take more action.

At times, you may feel you're not on the right track. It's possible that your current path will make more sense later and that you'll use skills and talents for a new, possibly happier direction.

I asked Jennifer Puckett, another successful friend, to share how she paved the way for her life purpose. Her story shows not only how you can arrange your life and get support to make your calling work for you, but also that your past can be a great transition to the next leg of your journey.

Jennifer's Story

My life was forever changed by the birth of my gorgeous son—forever changed in the most fabulous way you can imagine. I love being a mom, but it altered how I look at everything in life, including work. Prior to having my son, I was a full-time musician, the lead singer of both a band and a duo act. I didn't have the glamorous rock-and-roll lifestyle that you read about, but I was having a ball chasing my dream, supporting myself financially doing what I love.

Later, I met my husband and became pregnant. As a result, I knew that my life had to change. I couldn't continue the late nights, little pay, drunk companions, and crazy life on the road. I realized that after five years, it was time for a change, so I went back into a former job.

Eventually, I found myself dragging my feet every day just to make it to work. I knew two things in my heart: 1) I wanted to be home with my baby, and 2) even though I had "grown up," it was hard for me to go back into a box after living my dreams and experiencing life at its fullest. So I decided to leave the job and stay at home with my son. I had discovered while working as a musician that I was extremely good at techie stuff. I often built websites for agencies and businesses to supplement my income during our slow times.

Looking back at everything, I can see how I was being prepped for where I am at now! Little did I know that after taking the first step to leave my job, everything would fall into place. I would soon operate a successful business as a virtual assistant, doing work that I love, getting the pleasure of collaborating with other like-minded, outside-the-box thinkers, even using my creative skills to grow businesses besides my techie ones.

Although at times I feel like I want to pull my hair out balancing being a mom, wife, and business owner, I wouldn't have it any other way. I get to be me! That's so important, since it can be way too easy to forget who you are when you're dealing with the corporate grind day in and day out, trying to conform to who your employer thinks you should be. That life is just not for me.

Working from home and being a stay-at-home, groovy type of mom can definitely have its challenges. Honestly, I don't know if I balance it well, but I do the best I can. I think that's all anyone can do. I think it's just a matter of doing what works for you and your family.

Guidance for You Along the Way

You might be wondering at this point how you too can find your purpose. Try to think of your search as a process, and know that your reasons for being will evolve with you. If you feel stuck, remember that it's only temporary. In my work as a professional psychic, one of the most common questions I receive is "What is my life purpose?" So rest assured that you're not alone.

To ease the way a bit, I will share the most-mentioned guidance that has come through for my clients. This information comes from giving hundreds of readings to rebel chick mystics asking about their life purposes:

1. Understand that it's up to *you* to figure out a path that works for you. You may be like some of my clients, expecting me to tell you what your life purpose is. As I tell them, you might not feel that you know what you're meant to do, but chances are, you really do know it in your heart. I can give you some general information about the essence of your mission here, but the way you fulfill it is your choice. You have so many options—I've never seen anything set in stone about how you need to go about accomplishing things.

2. Think in terms of general themes. When working with clients, I will hear a phrase that's short and to the point. For example, my own life purpose phrase is "to empower women to live authentic lives." I could fulfill this in a number of ways, in a number of professions. Although my jobs have differed tremendously, I always found that core idea was present in my work. It might take you a while to figure out your own theme, but you don't have to know it to be living it already, perhaps through volunteer work or helping friends and family. It doesn't have to involve a job or career.

3. Look at your hobbies. For example, you might be a musician, working on writing songs that are healing for women. Some people might consider your music to be something that you just do for fun. Even if you don't get paid for it yet, being a musician could be your life purpose if that feels right for you. (I'll talk more about money and life purpose later in this chapter.)

4. Your life purpose often answers the age-old question, "Why am I here?" The answer is always individual and personal. It's about following the path of your heart, usually involving your passions.

5. Although I consider your job, career, calling, and life purpose to be separate things, they are usually also related. It can be helpful for you to look at them individually to form a complete picture of your purpose.

Exercise: Beginning to Identify Your Purpose and Calling

In your journal, answer the following two questions:

1. What is my life purpose?

2. What is my calling?

Put down the first things that come to you. If you need to write a lot to get some clarity, be sure to give yourself plenty of time. Remember that your answers are not set in stone, and they might change later. Try not to think about whether you're living your purpose and calling right now. If you feel that you aren't on the right track, you will stop yourself from allowing your inner truth to come out.

Just as with your purpose, your calling can be expressed in a number of ways. You might do small acts of kindness each day for strangers, send love and prayers to a war-torn area of the world, or feed a stray cat. My calling is to help women become more courageous. This manifests in a number of ways, from encouraging a client to start her own business to assisting a friend in setting up her blog to just being a cheerleader for friends and family through phone calls and e-mails.

Quiz: Is Your Career Path a Job, Calling, or Purpose?

Later in this chapter, you'll create an action plan to live more of your calling and purpose. This quiz will get you started by helping you see how your current career situation fits in so that you can know what you need to do to move forward with your purpose. (Please note that if you are a housewife or mom, you have an important career, so please still complete the quiz.) This is just an assessment tool, not intended to create additional worries or stress for you.

Think of your career path as you answer this quiz. Place a check mark by the statements that fit you the best:

- ❑ *I feel inspired by my work.*
- ❑ *I enjoy my work.*
- ❑ *I love making the world a better place.*
- ❑ *I like making a difference.*
- ❑ *I enjoy helping others.*
- ❑ *I am energized by being of service.*
- ❑ *I love helping people heal themselves.*
- ❑ *I wake up each morning excited about my day.*
- ❑ *I use my creativity in my job.*
- ❑ *I look forward to going into work.*
- ❑ *I enjoy finding solutions for others.*
- ❑ *I find time to follow my passions.*
- ❑ *I would do my work even if I wasn't paid for it.*
- ❑ *I like to inspire others.*
- ❑ *I have energy to pursue hobbies and interests outside of my profession.*

Answer key: Look to see how many check marks you have. The more sentences you marked, the more chance there is that you're following your calling or purpose with your career path. If you don't have more than a few, you might need to look closer at whether your job serves your true self. Consider making a list in your journal of the various ways that your current work helps you to serve your calling or purpose. This might require some creative thinking.

You may still be asking, "What if I don't know what my life purpose or calling is?" Consider that you could be missing the obvious. Let's say you're a musician who loves to entertain people—actually, it's your passion. If you told me about this, I'd describe your purpose as "to entertain people with music." Your calling might be similar: "to bring harmony and enjoyment to the world." Yet you might protest, saying that you're a schoolteacher or telling me that "music won't pay the bills."

I challenge you to think in different ways. Chances are, you bring your musical essence to the classroom in your day job, even if you don't teach music as a subject. It's who you are, most likely informing a great portion of what you do in your life, including your career. You also have options to make your day job, calling, and life purpose intersect. You could teach music, possibly changing careers, or you give lessons in your spare time. You also could sell your music and get paid to perform.

I brainstorm with my clients to get some ideas about how to bring life purpose and calling more into daily life. You can do the same on your own or with others—perhaps members of a group you join, inspired by Chapter 8. If you still feel stuck, don't worry. You will have some clarity eventually. In the meantime, let your inner child come out to play, to help you figure this out.

What Do You Want to Be When You Grow Up?

When you were a kid, well-meaning adults probably asked you, "What do you want to be when you grow up?" Chances are, you answered them enthusiastically—no one had told you yet that you were unrealistic for wanting to be a ballerina, doctor, clown, writer, or astronaut. You didn't doubt it, until someone asked, "Who do you think you are?" With that question, unhappy adults with low self-esteem were trying to crush your dreams, asking you what made you think you can do those big, amazing things with your life.

Lea recounted her experience with this earlier in the chapter, and I also recall adults steering me away from a creative career (in my case, being a writer), saying it wouldn't pay much. Well, no one knew back then that the Internet would develop the way it has, creating many more opportunities for writers. I worked on other career paths for sure, but still ended up writing professionally. Sometimes your life purpose might seem to get lost, but it's possible to reclaim it.

Limiting things that the grown-ups told you while you were younger were really unfair. But since you're an adult now, you don't have to let that negativity run and ruin your life. You can make your own choices now. When someone asks, "Who do you think you are?" you can tell them that you're just getting started and plan to do even more. I give you full permission to rebel against others' negativity. Let's begin by going back to your childhood to rewrite your story specifically regarding what you want to be when you grow up.

Exercise: What Do You Want to Be Now?

Children love to have fun, tending to live in the moment more than adults do. For this reason, kids can be excellent teachers, especially when it comes to life purpose. When you feel stuck in the adult mind-set of working hard all the time, you miss out on playing or having fun, thereby accessing your creativity. Right now, it might seem like figuring out what you want to be when you grow up is a process that requires some mature common sense. You have bills to pay, and you need to keep a roof over your head, along with food on the table.

But using your creative or childlike side to find your life purpose can be fun, as well as producing results where previous exercises may not have been successful. Kids very rarely think of why something can't happen or be done. They figure out ways to make things happen. Look at children who build forts in the living room to have their own space or construct their own rocket ships for going to the moon. Growing up, I even had a friend who found a bicycle that someone had thrown away and fixed it up, actually manifesting a bike he wanted in the end. The sky is the limit for children.

Before you begin responding to the prompts that follow, think about yourself as a young girl. Picture the age when you knew who you were, along with what you wanted to be when you grew up. Remember what you confidently said when asked about it. Take your time as you move forward with the exercise, as it might bring up difficult feelings and emotions. (Feel free to return to this exercise later or skip it altogether, if you feel clear about your purpose right now, or simply want to wait until you do further growth work.)

1. Write down the answer to the question, "What did you want to be when you grow up?" Record everything that comes to mind. Don't worry if it seems unrealistic or impractical right now. Let your younger self guide you for a bit, and listen to what comes through.

2. Compare what you wrote for Step 1 to your dreams today. Do your current goals and vision correspond in any way to those of your younger self? If it doesn't feel like it, or you feel as though you're on an opposing path, you may wish to use your creativity to discover similarities or connections.

3. Write down the ways in which your current career path, along with your purpose and calling, resemble those early desires. If any childhood negativity arises, be sure to check in with yourself. Focus on how you've since turned around damaging beliefs or harmful messages, giving yourself love and credit.

4. Write down a humorous, healing story about all of the jobs and career situations that didn't work out for you. You might use a first-person, factual narrative, or you might tell it as fiction with you as the protagonist, interacting with other interesting characters. Use your creativity and humor to give your employment history. When you feel that it's complete, move on to the remaining steps.

5. Make a list of the things that you discovered about yourself from writing the story in Step 4. Write down the positive and more difficult lessons that you learned.

6. What strengths do you have that no one knows about?

7. Which new story do you want to tell about career and life purpose? How do you want the next ten years to look? What about the next 20 years? How will you still be of service in retirement? Write all of it down.

It's Not about the Money

After completing the previous exercise, you may find yourself worried that you can't mold your current situation according to your life purpose. If so, look at what's holding you back the most. For some of my clients, a main concern is this: "Will I be able to make enough money to support myself if I follow my dreams?" Your vision may seem like a luxury that you can't afford. Yet sometimes the divine has a way of getting your attention when you chase the money in your quest to find your life purpose, instead of doing what will make you happy.

I asked Leah Shapiro, one of my personal coaches, to share her profound wake-up call on this matter.

Leah's Story

Something had to change. I was stressed out, pissed off, and unhappy in my restaurant job. I knew that there was something more for me, but I had no idea what it was. I just knew that I was unhappy and unfulfilled, and that I wanted things to be different. Every now and then, I saw someone who seemed super shiny, with a twinkle in her eyes. I knew that I wanted some of what those people had. I just didn't know how to access it.

The problem was that I was hooked into the money that I made, feeling trapped. This made me angry, so I spent a lot of time blaming everyone else for my unhappiness. I also spent tons of time trying to fill the gaping hole of dissatisfaction. I was a big consumer of anything that would make me feel better. I partied like a rock star and spent tons of money trying to make myself happy.

This worked for a while, but I always ended up feeling dissatisfied and pissed off again. One day, exhausted from working too much over the holidays, I went into work to look at my schedule, hoping to have a few days off the next week. I discovered that I was scheduled for six shifts, instead of the three that I was hoping for. This scheduling issue pushed me over the edge! As I was overwhelmed with frustration, I declared loudly to the universe: "I just need a break!" Little did I know that the universe was listening.

I headed out to do a few errands prior to my next shift, stopping at the grocery store to pick up a few things. As I was walking out to my car, shopping bags in hand, I stumbled off the curb into a big dramatic fall in the street. I picked myself and my groceries up out of the middle of the road, hobbling to my car. By the time I got home, I knew something was seriously wrong with my ankle.

A trip to the emergency room confirmed that I had broken my foot and severely sprained my ankle. I was going to be out of work a minimum of six weeks. I had gotten the break I asked for!

For the first two weeks, I was forced to stay off my ankle and foot. This meant lying around doing nothing, which was new for me. For the past ten years I had been working nonstop. My new free time was exactly what I needed, though, in order to reevaluate my life. It was clear that I had to get out of the restaurant business. It wasn't working for me. One injury could put my whole livelihood at risk.

During my recovery, I read the books *The Four Agreements* and *The Mastery of Love,* both by Don Miguel Ruiz. They changed the way I was looking at everything. I realized that people weren't trying to piss me off or hold me back. I saw that I was responsible for my life. Those books started me down a path to self-discovery and spiritual awakening.

During my time off, I also watched Dr. Phil McGraw on Oprah Winfrey's show. I resonated with the way he that he put responsibility for life back into a person's lap, asking questions such as, "How's that working for you?" or "What are you going to do about that?"

The seed was planted for me to become a life coach. Within six months, I left the restaurant business, starting to work at a new job doing behavior modification with kids. I eventually moved on to go to coaching school. I also embarked on a two-year journey taking a spiritually based women's leadership course, which helped me get in touch with my neglected, non-conforming soul. I worked on creating my life to be the perfect reflection of the woman that I had become. Now, I'm happy to say that my life is totally kick-ass!

Leah's story shows that thinking too much about money can hold you back in finding your life purpose. Some rebel chick mystics report having similar wake-up calls that gently—or not-so-gently—forced them into finding options that made them feel happier and more fulfilled. Lessons that help you find your life purpose don't have to be difficult, though. Remember what you discovered in Chapter 7, that you can drop out of the School of Hard Knocks at any time.

Exercise: Life Purpose with Freedom, Not Financial Fear

Instead of creating crisis moments, you can examine the money issue in your journal to see where you may need to make changes. Write down the answers to the following questions:

1. If money were no object, how would you spend your life?

2. Do you believe that you have to make money before you can follow your dreams?

3. If you weren't so worried about earning a living, saving for the future, and finances in general, how would you spend a typical day? What would your lifestyle look like? What activities would you be doing? Who would you be spending time with?

4. How would you feel if money were not an issue?

In answering these questions, you might be surprised that you don't necessarily want to live on a tropical island, sipping umbrella drinks all day long. (Or maybe you do—after all, it's *your* life purpose that we're talking about.) You have full permission to dream big. One area for positive rebellion is to let go of others' ideas that what you want is frivolous, unrealistic, or unattainable. Perhaps naysayers have told you, "Be realistic!" or "Get real!" Take their words as an invitation to make your dreams a reality!

Exercise: Let Your Heart Lead You to Your True Purpose

I've discovered that sometimes we're not allowing our hearts to lead us. When working with rebel chick mystics, I always ask them to get really honest about their true desires.

I've already had you write down your life purpose in a prior exercise. But this time around, I'm going to ask you to be more honest! Chances are, you may have put down what you thought you should. You might not have been working from your heart. This is okay. Don't be too hard on yourself. Just take your journal and write down answers to the following prompts, especially if you think you may not have been as forthright as you could have.

1. What is your *true* life purpose? Think about how it might differ from your current job or career, but don't get stuck in these details.

2. Write down a list of ideas, brainstorming about how you can make your life purpose, job, and career intersect more. Be creative, calling upon your inner child to help guide you to your best answers.

3. What excites you the most about your real purpose?

Exercise: Creating Your Life-Purpose Action Plan

You're here to rock the world, not sit on the sidelines. Successful people usually set goals and take steps to accomplish them. At times, this advice has really annoyed me, even though it's useful. I wanted to accomplish everything on my lists today! But that's not possible.

As I've emphasized throughout this book, small steps are helpful in charting a new course. For example, you don't lose 20 pounds or more overnight. You drop weight pound by pound. It's the little things you do each day that add up to get the results you desire.

It's similar with life purpose. For example, you can't write a book in one sitting, create a successful business in one day, or master art or music in a month. In prior chapters, we worked on getting you some help to free up more time for what matters to you. So let's continue on this path of structuring your life even more, especially around your purpose.

If you're more of a big-picture person, the details of making plans sometimes get lost. I know you're busy, too, making it tough to keep up with everything. Follow these steps to make sure nothing falls through the cracks:

1. In your journal, write down all of your goals and dreams regarding your purpose. Make a master list of everything that's a part of it. Don't be afraid to think big.

2. Next, look at your lists, along with the answers to the other exercises and quizzes in this chapter to get a more complete picture of your purpose.

3. Circle your top five goals. Under each one, put down the actions required to make them a reality. It can feel overwhelming to write it all out. You might worry that you'll never find the time to get it all done. Remember that you won't have to do everything at once. Record each step, doing your best to not combine things. You want to make it easy to follow the plan.

4. Examining the action steps, identify one to three things that you can do on a daily basis to help you accomplish the major goals. For example, if you want to write a book, your three things might be a making a journal entry to juice up your creativity as you start your day, spending 10 to 15 minutes brainstorming ideas that can later be organized into an outline, and then writing 500 words for your book.

5. Figure out a system that works for you to assign yourself tasks. You can use pen and paper, creating lists to hang up in your work space or to carry with you in your purse or briefcase. I created a physical notebook, divided into my five major life areas. Under each one, I have a list of all of my goals for that area. I also include affirmations or other inspirational items. I assign tasks to myself each day, week, month, and year, putting them on my calendar. You might choose to use technology such as reminder applications for your mobile phone to help you stay on track each day. Enlist the support of a life coach if you need help with getting organized, or ask a loving, trusted friend who's systematic and thorough to give you some pointers on time management and scheduling tasks.

6. Find a way to be accountable. You could ask someone to be available for you to check in with on a daily basis to see if you did your steps, or it might be enough for you to put a check mark by the items each day or delete them from your electronic device.

Your daily actions might change as you accomplish your goals, since you'll have to pick new items for the top five to replace the ones you've reached (congratulations!). Honor the way that you prefer to work on things, too, since you might find it better to tackle one goal at a time versus all five at once.

Experiment to see what works for you. If you feel excited after making an action plan, this is a sign that you're on the right path. If you're not enthusiastic, try not to be hard on yourself. Perhaps you need additional time to figure out more about your purpose.

As for me, I smile since one of my actions is to remember to breathe. I enjoy starting my day with meditation, which helps me with this item. I find that having a spiritual practice is a necessity for me, not a luxury.

Of course, carving out your own spiritual path is an incredibly important aspect of being a rebel chick mystic—it's the *mystic* part of your journey. The healing work that you've done so far (from this book and in any other way) has addressed your spirit, which is key, since it frees up energy in your being to rock the world in your own, special way. The final chapter will discuss how you can continue to carve out your own spiritual path, offering you ideas, guidance, and inspiration.

Chapter Nine

Carve Out Your
Own Spiritual Path

*"The spiritual path, then, is simply the journey
of living our lives. Everyone is on a spiritual path,
most people just don't know it."*

— MARIANNE WILLIAMSON

Much of this book so far has focused on helping you
heal and rebel in positive ways. If you've done the exercises and quizzes, you have compiled your own rebel chick
mystic's guide. This chapter helps you to bring everything
together so that you can define and carve out your own
spiritual path.

This doesn't have to be complicated or time-consuming.
I believe that as women, we are especially and even natu-
rally connected to the divine since we have the ability
to bring new life into the world, similar to the beliefs in
earth-based spirituality. Like Marianne Williamson in the
quote that opens this chapter, I believe that everyone is on

a spiritual path in some way, a unique journey to the divine. According to Robert C. Fuller, the author of *Spiritual, But Not Religious,* some Americans consider themselves to be on this type of journey versus following a traditional religion. A humorous look at the difference between spirituality and religion that I enjoy very much comes from a 2005 *Newsweek* interview with singer-songwriter Bonnie Raitt. She was quoted as saying in concert, before playing one of her more spiritual songs, "Religion is for people who are afraid to go to hell. And spirituality is for those of us who have been there and back."

I honor that you may have some leanings toward traditional religion or organized spiritual paths. I've noticed that some women take the parts of their past or chosen religion, combining it with their personal spiritual practices such as meditation or yoga.

Earlier, I suggested that you could identify yourself as a mystic, using modern challenges and personal lessons as part of your healing without having to live in a temple, ashram, or monastery full-time. Rebel chick mystics usually live *in* the world, not apart from it. However, it can be entertaining, insightful, and inspiring to study the female mystics of the past. For example, although I'm not Catholic, I enjoy stories about the female saints' lives, especially when it comes to their rebellious side. I'm inspired by St. Catherine, who assisted Joan of Arc, whom she felt was a kindred spirit since they were both rebels who had divine visions. St. Catherine even rebelled against an emperor, revealing insights about him publicly that weren't so flattering, and converted others to her religion, including her persecutors. St. Bernadette is another who risked persecution. She said she was told by Mother Mary to dig a hole, which later became the popular healing springs of Lourdes.

These types of stories illustrate that women of the past have been called to do something important, possibly breaking the rules to do so. Even today, women in some countries must obey religious laws or face punishment and even death. If you don't face danger as you rebel along your spiritual path, you are very fortunate. But if you have felt wounded or excluded in less severe ways by traditional religion, you might still be cautious about carving out your own spiritual path. Doing so, however, is a form of positive rebellion. You can make your own rules and choose to honor your own heart and spirit in the process, instead of an outside authority.

Even if you don't feel like you are doing anything revolutionary, it's still possible to lead by positive example, whether it's your loving actions or the happy attitude that you radiate out to others. Being peaceful and upbeat in a sometimes-negative world is rebellious. I absolutely adore those bumper stickers that say ENLIGHTEN UP. I believe it's important to have some fun, joy, and happiness on the spiritual path. So I tend to use my own level of happiness as a meter to determine my success.

Some seekers have the goal of enlightenment, which means different things for different people. For one person, it might mean the end of suffering. For others, it's the ability to handle life's challenges with ease and grace, or a state of mind that's so peaceful that they can feel the interconnectedness of all things and people. Some teachers say that by finding and embracing your true self, you feel more connected to the divine, harmonizing with life and the universe.

No matter what your quest looks like, you have everything you need within you, as well as the conditions and resources necessary to reach your spiritual goals. You have the positive qualities of strength, courage, creativity, and a loving heart to tap into whenever you desire.

Choosing a Spiritual Teacher

Although I strongly believe that you are your own best authority, it still can be helpful to find a teacher to work with formally. Keep your preferences and personal style in mind as you're shopping around as a spiritual consumer. Even though information overload has spread to this part of life, the nice thing is that it's easier to access teachers and their wisdom due to so many technological advances, including podcasts, blogs, and online videos, articles, books, and classes. We also can travel more easily to meet our mentors these days.

Exercise: Choosing Your Teacher

If you are interested in formal spiritual studies, be an informed consumer. If something doesn't feel right, honor and trust your intuition. If anyone asks you to give up all of your money and possessions or requires you to have sex with him or her in order to receive teachings, you probably want to run in the other direction.

These things might sound obvious right now, but the spiritual path can sometimes make you drop your guard. You open up your heart, and sadly, some teachers try to take advantage of you. It has happened to some really smart, loving people, even in situations that don't fit typical cultlike conditions.

Do not judge yourself if this has happened to you. Instead, have compassion for yourself, mixed with oodles of tender loving care. You've most likely learned important things about whom to trust.

If any of this worries you, please answer the list of questions below in your journal to help you see if a teacher is a good fit. (In this exercise, I use "they," "them," and "their" in order to avoid excessive repetition of the awkward "he or she," "him or her," and "his or her" constructions.)

- Is the spiritual teacher walking their talk? Do they practice what they preach? Is their life consistent with their teachings? Do they have integrity?

- Is the spiritual teacher loving? Are they caring even when pointing out areas that need improvement? How do they treat their staff, loved ones, and other students?

- Is the spiritual teacher giving back to the world? Is this important to you or not? Do they donate their time or money to causes? If so, what do they support? Does it resonate with you?

- Is the spiritual teacher happy? (This is the most important thing to consider!)

- Is the spiritual teacher welcoming to everyone? Or is their circle very exclusive? Are teachings hidden or kept from you? Do you have to prove yourself before you'll be fully accepted into their circle?

- Is the spiritual teacher encouraging students to conform in acting or looking a certain way? If you do not conform, how does the teacher feel about this?

- Is the spiritual teacher also a student? Who are the teacher's mentors? What did they believe? Does the teacher just recycle the knowledge, or do they have their own spin on it?

- Is the spiritual teacher down-to-earth, or do they seem like they're trying to be a holy figure? Do they embrace their humanity?

- Is the spiritual teacher humorous at times? Or do they take life and themselves too seriously?

- Is the spiritual teacher someone who helps you feel better about life? Do you feel as though you're on the right path as you study with them?

- Is the spiritual teacher okay with being challenged? Or do you feel that you have to agree with everything that the teacher says or writes about?

- Is the spiritual teacher honest? Do they profess to know everything? Does the teacher acknowledge their own areas of growth?

- Is the spiritual teacher overly concerned about money? Do they charge reasonable fees for teachings or materials? How does the teacher handle those who cannot afford to study with them?

- Is the spiritual teacher encouraging you to eventually become your own guide?

- Is the spiritual teacher accessible at least by e-mail? Are they open to questions from students?

Your answers may be quite interesting. When I formulated those questions myself, I thought about the positive qualities of the many spiritual teachers that I've studied with. I've only had a couple of negative experiences, and they didn't turn me off from the idea of formal instruction.

On the other hand, you may not want to study with a teacher at this time, and that's okay. Without undertaking official studies, you still have instructors in human form, such as your spouse, family members, co-workers, boss, and friends, or even people you meet as you go about your day. They help you learn about love as you carve out your own spiritual path. It seems as though we're all spiritual teachers *and* students simultaneously.

The idea of being a spiritual teacher sometimes intimidates rebel chick mystics, and some of them have said things like, "Who me? What do I have to offer others?" I believe that all women have important wisdom to share with others. As you live in the world, not apart from it, your unique contributions will emerge. As you learn to trust yourself, you may start to notice how different teachers just confirm what you know to be true in your heart. You will become aware and inspired when it comes to your own gifts, talents, and lessons learned.

At times, you may desire to teach what you've learned to others. As I emphasized earlier, you can impart this wisdom by just the way that you lovingly lead by example. Or you might decide to actively go out and mentor, coach, heal, or inspire others. Whatever path you choose, all types of teachers are needed in the world.

Exercise: Which Type of Spiritual Teacher Are You?

Take your journal and write a few paragraphs about what type of spiritual teacher you are. Include such details as whether you like to teach by example, formally, in groups, one-on-one, in person, with individuals you already know, with new people, or even via the Internet. What do you enjoy the most about teaching others? How does teaching others inspire you?

Write down everything that comes to mind. The things that you write down here can be helpful to turn to for inspiration during times of self-doubt, if you wonder if you make a difference. Or, if formal opportunities arise for you to teach, you can see if they are in alignment with your style of being a spiritual teacher. Honor that you might just prefer an indirect style of teaching. Some rebellious types avoid interactions with others. This is sometimes due to being sensitive to energies or not knowing how to manage them.

Energies and Rebel Chick Mystics

So far, this book has given you tools and ideas to help you start taking better care of yourself, and managing energies is another form of self-care. Some rebel chick mystics are criticized or judged by others for being "too sensitive." Some say, "I wear my heart on my sleeve." Many of these women are lovely souls with amazing gifts and skills. Some are talented and loving writers, musicians, artists, and healers; others have big hearts, caring deeply about the people in their lives or the fate of the planet. In personal relationships, these sensitive women give so much love to others that it depletes their life force.

In some cases, I've helped others just to alleviate their pain or suffering so that I wouldn't have to feel it! I definitely used to have an overly developed sense of empathy, sometimes called being an energy empath. In psychic circles, this is known as *clairsentience*. It means "clear feeling," and describes getting intuitive guidance in the form of emotions, bodily sensations, and energetic changes.

No matter what your sensitivity level is, it can be very tiring to make your relationships the top priority. When you feel others' energies, including their emotions, it can be overwhelming. You may feel so drawn to assist them, sharing the tools, techniques, and wisdom you've gathered from carving out your own spiritual path. But if you don't take care of yourself in the process, you risk burning out, which prevents you from having the energy and motivation to follow your passions, purpose, and calling. Please know that it's still possible to live in a heart-centered way and help others without ending up drained.

Still, it can make you feel as though you're different, especially if others don't seem to understand. I invite you to see your sensitivity, regardless of its level, as a gift and blessing. If you feel guided to do so, you can write down in your journal the many ways that it serves you. Here are some examples to get you started:

- *I'm more in touch with my intuition or inner knowing.*

- *I'm able to pick up on subtle nuances while learning a new song, dance, or artistic technique.*

- *I can avoid foods and chemicals that aren't healthy for me.*

- *I am in touch with my body, mind, and spirit.*

- *I know when someone needs a hug or a listening ear.*

- *I find joy and beauty in the simple things in life.*

- *I'm forced to take good care of myself.*

- *I can sense and protect myself from the harsh energies.*

- *I can enjoy the restorative energies of nature, since I'm tuned in to the subtler side of life.*

Following are some ideas that I've developed in working with rebel chick mystics who need help with managing energies. This list is not exhaustive. As you use these methods or your own, you may find that you still get tired or drained at times, but the frequency or intensity could lessen. You will want to find what works for you. Depending on what you have going on, you may have to tweak your energy-management routine or tools from time to time. But really, this doesn't have to be complicated. In fact, you might notice that some of the following methods are simple self-care routines.

Tools and Methods to Manage Energy Sensitivity

1. Grounding. Do a visualization exercise, imagining roots coming out of your feet into the earth. This helps you feel focused and less likely to get off-kilter when stress or harsh energies occur.

2. Shielding. You can visualize a bubble of your favorite color as a protective shield. Experiment with what colors work best for you, or even layer different shades. Shielding helps you understand what is your stuff (emotions, feelings, and energies) versus someone else's stuff.

3. Sea-salt baths. Sprinkle some sea salt into your bathwater and soak in the tub. This will cleanse the energies that you might have picked up during the day.

4. Aura sprays. You can buy these at metaphysical stores or find instructions online or in energy-healing books for making your own. Aura sprays can contain gems, herbs, or essential oils with different intentions. They can help with protection, clearing, abundance, physical energy, mental clarity, and relaxation.

5. Intention. As you start each day, intend to only encounter loving, kind people. Expect to let negativity just roll off you like water on a high-tech fabric. Plan to be energized by your interactions with others.

6. Healthy living. Eat well, exercise, practice yoga, meditate, use stress-management techniques, repeat affirmations, and relax. If you're feeling good, less negativity will be attracted to you, and you'll feel more confident in your ability to let things go.

7. Bodywork or energy work. Touch is healing and relaxing. Plus, you get to take time for yourself, enabling you to reduce stress so that you're able to function better.

8. Breathe. Sometimes when you're rushed or busy, your breathing pattern changes as your physical body tightens up. Inhaling and exhaling deeply helps clear the energies you might have picked up. It also relaxes you. You may want to take some classes on breathing techniques such as pranayama, which comes from yoga.

9. Cord cutting. Spiritual author Doreen Virtue writes and teaches about having Archangel Michael cut the ties that no longer serve you. The theory is that sometimes people (even those you love) attach a cord of energy to you, often unintentionally. These can drain you over time. By keeping just the loving energies, you'll feel clearer and suffer less interference from others. Before I started to do this, it felt as though I could hear people's thoughts running in my head after we visited. I don't get as tired from interactions since I cut my cords now.

10. Detachment. Being detached doesn't mean that you don't care. It just means that you don't allow yourself to get sucked into someone else's drama. You don't try to fix them or stop them from making mistakes, even though you might clearly see that they are going down a path of self-destruction. As they advocate in the recovery movement, you love the person, but you don't love their harmful behavior. You can be there and listen. You can provide help if they ask and seriously want it. But you don't expend effort to get them to change or to fix them in any way. By detaching, you free up tons of energy to do more important things, such as work on your goals, projects, and dreams.

11. Get support. When you feel overwhelmed, write about it in your journal, talk to a trusted friend, or go to a counselor or other healing professional. Say some prayers to your divine helpers, asking for assistance. This is another reminder to not get caught up in the DIY lie! Allowing yourself to receive support is a powerful form of self-love.

The Ultimate Form of Positive Rebellion

I consider one of the main goals of your spiritual path to be loving yourself more. When you love yourself more, it can set off a positive chain reaction, beginning by helping you become happier. When you're happier, you're in a better place to help others. By assisting others, you alleviate suffering in the world, possibly increasing collective happiness. So caring for yourself is a good thing! Yet I've heard all kinds of objections when I mention loving yourself more. Here are some of the most common ones:

- *It's selfish to love myself more than others.*
- *I don't know how to love myself. I never learned how.*
- *I've done horrible things, and it's too hard to love myself.*
- *I can't love myself because I'm fat, ugly, or stupid* [or other negative adjectives].
- *I feel silly loving myself.*
- *I've tried and it has never worked for me.*
- *I don't have the time to work on this.*

These objections can be shifted over time with practice. You can rebel against a world that sends so many messages that you need to improve yourself to be considered lovable. You also hear that you're conceited or self-absorbed if you care for yourself. You've done lots of work on releasing these types of old beliefs. Try to continue and create a path where you love yourself as much as you can.

Each time you look in a mirror, love every cell and fiber of your being, telling yourself that you rock, are beautiful and amazing, or whatever makes you feel good. (Self-help icon and affirmation pioneer Louise L. Hay refers to this as *mirror work*.) The more you learn to love and take care of yourself, the more you will let go of your inner critics, becoming more inspired and happy, with more freedom to be your true self!

If this feels too difficult to embrace, again, it might help to think about how loving (or even just accepting) yourself makes it easier to care for others. There is another type of mirror work to consider here. Some popular spiritual teachers say that others are our mirrors, showing us both the positive and negative qualities in each other. The things that we don't approve of in others are the things that we haven't learned to love in ourselves.

I believe that if I work on loving and accepting myself, it can affect those I meet in a positive way. They get to see their good qualities mirrored back to them. The key is to not judge others for their so-called bad traits. When I'm tempted to condemn someone, I refer to this passage by Wayne Dyer in his book *You'll See It When You Believe It:* "I remind you again to keep in mind that when you judge another, you do not define that person, you define yourself."

Spiritual teachers have been saying that "we're all one" for ages. If it's true, then this work of loving yourself is especially important. Of course, it's up to you to define your spiritual path, according to your own terms, not just according to what popular leaders say. The next exercise will help you do so even more clearly.

Exercise: Create Your Path with a Vision Board

Even though this is a self-help book, my intention is to guide you to create your own spiritual path, versus telling you how to live. You're the expert out there about what is best for your life. I only can share what has worked for me and hope that it may inspire you. This is my personal formula for peace and happiness in life:

- *I try to keep things simple.*
- *I work on going within for my answers, with quiet reflection, journaling, meditation, or being in nature.*
- *I don't try to be perfect.*
- *I embrace my human side.*
- *I define happiness and success on my own terms.*
- *I practice self-love and self-acceptance.*
- *I work on being grateful, especially for difficult people, situations, and lessons.*
- *I do my best to let go of the past.*
- *I work on being happy now instead of waiting until later.*
- *I work on having as much fun and joy in my life as possible!*

This activity will help you define your spiritual path, too. Please note that you'll need to gather some supplies, so you may want to read through the exercise before beginning.

1. Make a vision board. You can use a poster board, corkboard, or virtual design space as your canvas. You might choose to use a tri-fold cardboard poster so that you can stand it up on your altar or other place you connect with spirit. Collect things that resonate with your spiritual path. Cut out photographs, pictures, or words, or find

sacred items that represent who you are spiritually and what your journey is all about.

Have some fun with this. Be sure to include fun things or even step outside your comfort zone. When I made a spiritual vision board for myself, it included representations of Catholic saints, the Hindu god Ganesh, Buddha, and modern spiritual teachers; my favorite words; pictures of my favorite guitars, the ocean, and yoga; affirmations; paper fortunes from fortune cookies; surfing photos; and magazine images of my favorite animals. Embrace your uniqueness!

2. Use your vision board to see where your spiritual interests are focused. Let it guide you to make a plan for creating daily practices. For example, you might notice that you have posted many photographs from nature. It might be that your spirit is guiding you to spend more time outside, relaxing or calming your mind. Perhaps you put up a bunch of photographs of people doing yoga. You may wish to try out yoga for the first time or make changes to your existing practice. If you notice that you have a few religious symbols from various traditions, these might be your spirit guiding you to study other paths to see which ones resonate with you.

3. Start incorporating the things you're drawn to into your daily life. You don't have to do it all. You can pick one or two things focus upon each day. Just do what feels good for you. What you choose will compose your spiritual path, as simple as that sounds.

4. Refer to and focus upon this vision board regularly, especially if you ever feel like you're not connected with

spirit. It will remind you of your true identity and your unique path. It can inspire you to connect with your higher self. Let that inspiration come from within, allowing it to surface in the moment, according to your needs.

Having a spiritual practice will affect other areas of your life as well, making them more enjoyable or manageable. You might find that it has an impact on how you reevaluate your priorities and plan for the future. It can be helpful to put things together so that you have a clear sense of who you are on all levels.

Putting It All Together

This is an exciting time! I wouldn't be a very good teacher of positive rebellion if I didn't help you create an overall statement from what you've learned. After all, manifestos are written by intellectuals, revolutionaries, and others who think outside the box. You have something important to say, too, but it's going to be about your own life, a much more personal creed.

I want you to go rock the world when you're done reading this book. We need your unique essence and contribution right now. My sincere hope is that you have found some clarity, along with a few tools to help you to move forward. If you feel any inherited limiting beliefs pop up after reading this book, be sure to toss them aside. You might choose to write them down and destroy the piece of paper. Remember that releasing the old energies that no longer serve you is a process, so be gentle with yourself.

You've done some hard work. Right now, I'd like you to take some time to look at all of the responses you made to the exercises as you read this book. Allow yourself to really bask in your greatness. You rock! Then give yourself a big hug, and get ready to write your very own manifesto for living your best possible, most inspired life.

Exercise: Writing Your Rebel Chick Mystic Manifesto

Write down a short, personal mission statement about your real self. This is your manifesto. Write about what you came to the planet to do for yourself and others. Put down who you are and what you believe. Keep an eye out for perfectionism. You can always add things as you think of them later, and you can recycle or reuse pieces that you wrote as you read this book. As I've always said, you are the authority in your own life, so you get to make your own rules.

Your Rebel Chick Mystic Manifesto can guide you in times of stress or worry. Refer to it if you ever have self-doubts, worries, or fears. It's a powerful way to connect to your true self and life purpose, and be reminded again of your spiritual path.

It felt powerful to create my own manifesto. I smiled as I read it, and I felt liberated. In the past, I might not have believed the wonderful things I wrote. I might have denied them or made fun of myself for thinking too big or being a dork. But because I like to walk my talk, I will bare my soul a bit, sharing my Rebel Chick Mystic Manifesto with you. Perhaps it will provide you with some inspiration and ideas.

I am a punk rock, rebel spirit here to rock the world. I'm a passionate writer who loves to empower women to live authentically. I'm a courage coach, catalyzing women to move forward and to take action on their dreams. I proudly wear my heart on my sleeve, loving most people in my life with all of my heart. I believe that by healing my spirit I'm part of a *revolution of love* that is going to help to shift and heal the world. Music is my life, my muse, my friend, my guide, and what sets me on fire. I'm a lovingly gentle warrioress. I prefer to live using my intuition and creativity. I simultaneously enjoy being a human being, woman, and spirit. I refuse to ever give up. I believe in following your heart, your dreams, and carving out your own path. I refuse to take myself too seriously. I embrace my true beauty, of being a nonconformist in the way I live, dress, and think. I believe in walking my talk. I believe that the only truth is your own. I believe in being open-minded, big-hearted, patient, and compassionate, especially with myself. I believe in doing all things with a bit of sass, style, humor, and grace. I believe the whole point of being on a spiritual path is to be happy. All of this is my mission. This is who I am. I am a rebel chick mystic.

I would absolutely love to read your own Rebel Chick Mystic Manifesto. Come over to my website at **www .lisaselow.com** to share it with me and others. Join the rebel chick mystic movement! We are waiting for you.

Afterword

*"Shoot for the moon. Even if you miss it,
you will land among the stars."*

—LES BROWN

As you end your journey here, please know that you are awesome. Chances are, you've learned some new things about yourself. Please, don't put this book on your shelf only to collect dust, and don't file away your journal— your very own rebel chick mystic guide. Refer to both, especially when you feel stuck, or if *crapitude* creeps up on you.

Most important, take action, even small steps. Don't wait for your dreams to come true—make them happen. You can do it! I also ask you to get help if you feel stuck. Be sure to check out my website, **www.lisaselow.com**, for additional resources and to connect with like-minded souls. I appreciate your sharing this book with other rebel chick mystics.

To be honest, I almost titled this book *A Rebel Chick Mystic Manifesto,* but I didn't want to it to seem like I was an authority on your life. I didn't want you to think that I was writing a manual that would tell you exactly how to live. Rather, I wanted you to see me as simply your facilitator of healing, clarity, and self-awareness. I thought it would be fun to lovingly coax you into writing your own rebel chick mystic guide (or manifesto, if you prefer). This resonated with my own rebel spirit. My intention is to start a new subculture of spiritual women who are here to make a difference. The world needs us to shine, sharing our gifts and talents with the world.

My hope is that your path is filled with much love and happiness. I also hope that you continue to discard your limiting beliefs and release the past, clearing the way for your true self to make its mark in the world. Please know that I'm on this journey with you, learning more about myself and finding my own way. Together, we can help to create peace and love on the planet.

When you make changes, you might notice that some people, even those you love, might not understand. But if you feel good and your heart is happy, it's a sign that you're on the right path. Keep on going! Those around you will follow your example when they are ready. Be loving, kind, and patient toward yourself and others as the healing changes occur. Even if your relationships shift in some way, the universe will support you. New people and things will come into your life as a result of your changes. You'll also gain fresh insights and ideas about your current relationships.

You are not alone. Many other women are working on becoming more of their true selves, living their purposes, and rocking the world. You are in good company. Please remember that you are so needed right now.

You have some empowering tools from this book to fuel the next phase of your journey. I invite and challenge you to continue to use them as you evolve. The most important thing is to enjoy your journey. I'm sending you many blessings, cheering you on from the sidelines. You can do anything that you set your heart, mind, and spirit to—and I can't wait to see what you accomplish!

Blessings,

Lisa Marie Selow

Acknowledgments

I'm so grateful to so many people for their love and support, not just during the writing of this book, but in other areas of my life. I apologize in advance if I inadvertently have left someone out. Please know that you're always in my gratitude- and love-filled heart.

First of all, I want to thank my hubby, Jan Selow, for always supporting me with my dreams. Not many people can say that they've been with their best friend and soul mate since age 21. Thank you for your love and patience, along with your willingness to grow on the spiritual path with me. Thanks so much for taking many of the domestic duties while I was writing, helping me learn more of my own lessons about how to receive better. I appreciate your tech help, back rubs, and French-press skills. Thanks for giving me your awesome pep talks when I felt nervous or worried. It's hard to put into words how much your support has helped me. I love you and look forward to us writing the next exciting chapter in our lives!

A special thanks to spirit for sending me so many beautiful animal friends who visited me frequently on the back porch during the writing of this book, such as my squirrel kids, and the opossum, raccoons, chipmunks, birds, skunks, and bunnies. Thank you, divine source for always leading the way!

I also want to thank the powerful, courageous line of women that I come from— especially my mom, Judy; my late maternal grandma, Edith; and the late Nana Clara— for inspiring me with their bravery and ability to love so deeply. I also thank the women on the Other Side who guide me, especially my great aunt Liz and one of my greatest mentors, Kathy Sinnett.

I especially want to thank Hay House for giving me this chance to get my message into the world to be of service. You helped me feel very welcome by greeting me with: "Welcome to the Hay House family." Your work has been pivotal in my own spiritual journey, and I'm so blessed that you are my publisher. Thank you to the entire Hay House family! Thank you, Louise Hay, for being a pioneer and rebelling by starting your own publishing company to do things your own way. I aspire to be like you when I grow up! Thanks to Cheryl Richardson and Reid Tracy for your belief in me. Thanks from my heart to my editor, Shannon Littrell, for your guidance and support—you rock! Thanks, too, to Christy Salinas for helping me get the most beautifully perfect book cover design—I fell in love with it. Also, thank you to designers Amy Rose Grigoriou and Riann Bender, and to the Hay House marketing team for your assistance, 'cause you rock!

A special thanks to both the Hay House Movers and Shakers and Writer's Workshop communities for your love and support. Thanks and love to Karen McCronklin for your support. You are the cheerleader for so many of us Movers and Shakers and Writer's Workshop participants. Thanks to rock-and-roll sister Michelle Buchanan for our fun banter about Girlschool, guitars, music, and writing. You all truly rock!

Lots of love, thanks, and hugs to my author gal pals: ReGina Norlinde, Erin Cox, Dawn Maslar, and Cathy Goulet for your support and love. Thanks to my many business gal pals and many blogging buddies, especially Michelle Amethyst Mahoney, Eleanor Ross, Michelle Shaeffer, Sherrie Koretke, Astra Spider, Claire Davis, Jean Kowalski, Morrighan Lynne, Paula Masterman, and Jeannine Luke Kenworthy for your support and cheerleading. Special thanks to my soul sisters who always have my back, especially Melissa Dalyrmple, Janice Olson, Connie Jordan, Carol Raab, Brigitte Parvin, Patty Shaw, and Kristy Reardon.

A special thanks to juicy, joyful Lisa McCourt for sharing your wisdom and guidance with me. Thanks for your giving heart and support!

Big thanks to Mona Lisa Schulz, M.D., Ph.D., for the transformative medical intuitive reading at the end of 2010. It helped me flex my courage muscles and get me out of my hermit's cave. Thank you for sharing spirit's guidance!

A special thanks and love to Jessica Kelley for your editorial assistance. I knew from the start that you were the perfect person for me to work with. I appreciate your hand-holding, cheerleading, support, hard work, patience, creativity, and special care. You are not only an editor, but a book midwife. Thanks so much for all of your help!

Thanks to Alyson Mead for all of your wonderful editorial assistance with my book proposal. Thanks, too, for your friendship and support! Infinite love and thanks to my "techista," the very talented Jennifer Puckett—you are a true friend, too, and I love you!

Hugs and love to Michelle Phillips for your guidance and coaching. Thanks for your support, especially when I had moments of freaking out! You are a sister of the heart. I'm so grateful for you. They always say that the teacher appears when you are ready. Thank you for your love and wisdom. A special shout-out to the Coaching Circle members, too. You are such amazing, powerful, and beautiful women! Thanks for your cheerleading and kind support in my journey.

Big, sassy love to Lisa Clark for your love and support and bringing out my more sparkly, author girl side. I always think of you as my soul sister. Thanks for blessing my path with your loads of friendship, wisdom, and hot pink!

Love, hugs, and thanks to my honorary big sister, Cindy Eyler. You've always been one of my biggest supporters. Your wisdom during my dark night of the soul kept me going on my path. You are such a gift, and you're an inspiring example of a rebel chick mystic. I'm so grateful to you and love you loads. Thanks for your support and checking in with me as I wrote this book.

Heartfelt thanks from deep within me to Doreen Virtue and the entire angel community of ATP©'s and Angel Intuitives for your many years of support with my life purpose and healing journey. You truly are my angel family! Thanks for keeping me on track and giving your love so freely!

A special thanks to Lama Marut for helping me "get medieval on my suffering" and for your many teachings that have fueled me for years. Many thanks to Lissa Rankin and Amy Ahlers for igniting me as a visionary. Tons of love and thanks to Amy Saari for helping me find my voice again on many levels. Love to Kate Northrup for inspiring me to live with more creativity, freedom, and abundance. Loads of love to Leah Shapiro—you're a kick-ass coach and mermaid. Special thanks to Gail Trauco for your friendship and mentoring—hugs to you, even though I know you prefer handshakes!

I especially want to thank my best friend, Lisa McEwen. Ever since ninth-grade gym class, you've been my honorary sister. Thanks for your love and support for so many years in all areas of my life. Thanks for our many girls' days, which usually involved shopping and/or cupcakes, along with our special brand of humor. I appreciate the e-mails, special cards, and chats, especially during the writing of this book. You helped me stay on course, remembering who I truly am—thank you! Here's to our perfection and being able to attend concerts until we're at least 100 years old.

To my dear soul sister Sharon Boury, thanks for your love and support. You are a fiercely loving, talented, and giving woman. You deserve all of the best that the universe desires to give you. Receive it all, baby! Thanks for our many long lunches and talks, along with supplying me with your beautiful flower essences and aura sprays to soothe my spirit, especially during my big life challenges and changes, as well during the writing of this book. I feel as though you are one of the ones who gets me. Thank you for everything! I always joke, "You are just too much." You truly are the best!

Special thanks and hugs and love to my honorary little sister, Eileen Brunelli. I always wanted a little sister and you are the best! Thank you for your support, cheerleading, angel readings, and love. More big hugs and love go out to another honorary sister, my friend Sue Tanida. Thank you for always being there for me and cheering me on—

you are so appreciated! Special thanks to my honorary little brother, Gabe, for your support and motivating me, along with keeping me informed about cool music. Great big hugs, love, and thanks to another honorary little brother, Chris Grosso, for your friendship, support, and inspiration as a friend and fellow author. Here's to dogma-free spirituality! Thanks and big love to my other honorary family, David and Deborah Kulp and Landon—I love you guys!

A special thanks to Sheldon Kay, the Rock and Roll Lawyer® and staff (especially rock-and roll-sister Elizabeth Quinto) for your guidance, support, and friendship. You guys truly *rock,* and I so appreciate your help. It was a joy to work with you. Here's to having a very wonderful life, filled with "Clarences."

A special thanks to everyone who provided endorsements and stories for this book. I'm so grateful for your willingness to support a new author on her path. Blessings and love to you!

I'm especially grateful to all of my clients throughout my career so far. Thanks for blessing my path and teaching me so much. It's wonderful to share this journey together. It's my desire for you to have only the best in life, always. I love you!

About the Author

Lisa Marie Selow is a motivational speaker, life coach, and modern mystic, specializing in liberating women to live with more courage and authenticity. She has a practical, down-to-earth, edgy, and humorous style as a spiritual teacher. Lisa says, "I like to bring a little bit of sass and spunk, glitter and glam, leather, rock-and-roll wisdom, and punk-rock attitude, mixed with generous helpings of love and laughter, to the spiritual and self-help fields."

Lisa's been a student of the healing arts since 1998, with prior career paths as a massage therapist, energy worker, and intuitive advisor. Prior to her "woo-woo" careers, she worked in the nonprofit and legal sectors due to her interests in social justice, environmental protection, and women's issues. These interests are still near and dear to her heart. In recent years, Lisa's work has shifted, combining her psychic and metaphysical side with an empowerment intention, focusing more on speaking and life coaching to assist other women's journeys.

Lisa lives in the Detroit area with her husband, Jan, along with several electric guitars. Her life and work have been heavily influenced by music, along with the inspiration of various countercultures throughout history. Lisa has a heart and soul of a rocker chick. Her passions are playing electric guitar, singing, attending live music shows, and being a student of music and life. Her heroines are rebellious women, from Joan of Arc to Joan Jett and everyone in between, including her late grandmother, Edith.

Lisa can be contacted at her website: **www.lisaselow.com**.

We hope you enjoyed this Hay House Insights book.
If you'd like to receive our online catalog featuring
additional information on Hay House books and products,
or if you'd like to find out more about the
Hay Foundation, please contact:

INSIGHTS

Hay House, Inc., P.O. Box 5100, Carlsbad, CA 92018-5100
(760) 431-7695 or (800) 654-5126
(760) 431-6948 (fax) or (800) 650-5115 (fax)
www.hayhouse.com® • **www.hayfoundation.org**

✫ ✫ ✫

Published and distributed in Australia by:
Hay House Australia Pty. Ltd., 18/36 Ralph St., Alexandria NSW 2015
Phone: 612-9669-4299 • *Fax:* 612-9669-4144 • www.hayhouse.com.au

Published and distributed in the United Kingdom by:
Hay House UK, Ltd., 292B Kensal Rd., London W10 5BE • *Phone:*
44-20-8962-1230 • *Fax:* 44-20-8962-1239 • www.hayhouse.co.uk

Published and distributed in the Republic of South Africa by:
Hay House SA (Pty), Ltd., P.O. Box 990, Witkoppen 2068
Phone/Fax: 27-11-467-8904 • www.hayhouse.co.za

Published in India by: Hay House Publishers India,
Muskaan Complex, Plot No. 3, B-2, Vasant Kunj, New Delhi 110 070
Phone: 91-11-4176-1620 • *Fax:* 91-11-4176-1630 • www.hayhouse.co.in

Distributed in Canada by: Raincoast, 9050 Shaughnessy St.,
Vancouver, B.C. V6P 6E5 • *Phone:* (604) 323-7100
Fax: (604) 323-2600 • www.raincoast.com

✫ ✫ ✫

Take Your Soul on a Vacation

Visit **www.HealYourLife.com®** to regroup, recharge,
and reconnect with your own magnificence.
Featuring blogs, mind-body-spirit news, and life-changing
wisdom from Louise Hay and friends.

Visit **www.HealYourLife.com** today!

Free e-newsletters
from Hay House, the Ultimate
Resource for Inspiration

Be the first to know about Hay House's dollar deals, free downloads, special offers, affirmation cards, giveaways, contests, and more!

 Get exclusive excerpts from our latest releases and videos from *Hay House Present Moments*.

 Enjoy uplifting personal stories, how-to articles, and healing advice, along with videos and empowering quotes, within *Heal Your Life*.

 Have an inspirational story to tell and a passion for writing? Sharpen your writing skills with insider tips from *Your Writing Life*.

Sign Up Now!

Get inspired, educate yourself, get a complimentary gift, and share the wisdom!

http://www.hayhouse.com/newsletters.php

Visit www.hayhouse.com to sign up today!

 HAY HOUSE

HAYHOUSE
RADIO

HealYourLife.com ♥